Billionaires for Bush

**Billionaires
for Bush**

How to Rule the World
for Fun and Profit

THUNDER'S MOUTH PRESS
NEW YORK

BILLIONAIRES FOR BUSH
HOW TO RULE THE WORLD FOR FUN AND PROFIT

Published by
Thunder's Mouth Press
An Imprint of Avalon Publishing Group Inc.
245 West 17th St., 11th Floor
New York, NY 10011

AVALON
publishing group incorporated

Library of Congress Cataloging-in-Publication Data is available.

ISBN 1-56858-324-9

9 8 7 6 5 4 3 2 1

Printed in Canada
Distributed by Publishers Group West

- Keep your mouth closed, as silence is gold, and gold is what we exist for;

- Collect our debts today. Pay the other fellow's debts tomorrow;

- Keep the seller waiting; the longer he waits, the less he'll take.
  Hurry the buyer, as his money brings us interest;

- Make all profitable bargains in the name of "Standard Oil," chancey ones
  in the names of dummy corporations;

- Never forget our legal department is paid by the year, and our land is full
  of courts and judges;

- As competition is the life of trade (our trade), and monopoly the death
  of trade (our competitor's trade), employ both judiciously;

- Never enter into a "butting" contest with the government. Our government
  is by the people and for the people, and we are the people, and those people
  who are not us can be hired by us;

- Always do "right." Right makes might, might makes dollars, dollars make
  right, and we have the dollars.

— Governing Rules of Standard Oil

CONTENTS

Chapter I: The Halls of Power

Chapter II: The Business

Chapter III: The Life

Welcome Aboard

MY FELLOW CHUMS AND FAR-FLUNG COLLEAGUES of inordinate wealth: I welcome you into the fold, the billfold of the upper sanctum. We run this country, and we do a damn good job of it. But for too long we have ruled from behind closed limo doors. The time has come to *step forward*, face America, and shamelessly be ourselves.

The book you hold in your hand, and the organization—dare I say social movement?—from which it springs, are more than a guide through the jungle of wealth and influence. Among these few pages resides our blueprint for the future. A future where policymakers are liberated from the shackles of "public interest," a future where no billionaire is left behind.

Billionaires for Bush—the political-action committee of CEOs, corporate lobbyists, dissolute heiresses, and other winners under George W. Bush's economic policies—is an exclusive club, for sure. But with this handy little manual we reveal, for the first time in paperback, the tips, tricks, and trade secrets that have led to our phenomenal success, including returns on our political investments of 100,000 percent and more.

It's not just about having that long row of zeroes behind your net worth. Any billionaire can do that. Rather, it is about an inbred comfort with graft, a well-developed sense of entitlement, and the moral sureness of vision that everything is for sale.

This book is of us, by us, and for us billionaires. Any of you Nascar dads and soccer moms, and even you quaint seven-figure upper-middle-class millionaires—don't even think about trying this stuff at home.

This is not a "how to" manual. It's a "how we did it" and a "how we're gonna keep doing it to you" manual. How did we get Dubya to pass three consecutive tax cuts that delivered $1.1 trillion of America's money into our pockets? It's here. How to secure no-bid contracts? How to eliminate overtime pay for eight million Americans and call it a victory for workers' rights? How to bring a Lear II in for a pinpoint on the double yellow while smashed on martinis? It's all here.

"There are two Americas," onetime Democratic presidential candidate John Edwards used to say. And who could quibble? We know this to be true better than anyone, because we are one of those Americas—and we own the other. We plan to keep it that way, and this book shows you how to *do it in style.*   — Phil T. Rich / Andrew Boyd

JOHN KASCHT

CHAPTER I

The Halls of Power

Billionaires for Bush

Where We Stand

OR THE GREATER PART OF THE 20TH CENTURY, democratic notions like "opportunity for all" and "public services" dominated the American political landscape. Government taxed the rich, regulated corporations, and protected the environment. The average person felt increasingly entitled to share in America's prosperity. Ordinary people were educated for free, and over 50 media companies competed to bring a balanced picture of what the government and corporations were up to.

Those were the dark days.

Since then, the billionaires have taken the reins. We used our money to beat democracy at its own game. In the early '70s we created think tanks like the Cato Institute, the American Enterprise Institute, and the Heritage Foundation. We paid scholars top dollar to invent theories explaining why increasing our wealth was in everybody's interest.

Next we found the perfect performer, Ronald Reagan, to sell our ideas. Boy, did he know how to charm. He nearly singlehandedly sold the middle classes on "trickle-down economics," the mythical golden shower.

Finally we bought up (and merged up) the media to ensure that our economic principles were the standard by which all policy must be judged.

Yes, we sure had a good run of it in the '80s. Unions were broken, industries were deregulated, public services were slashed, debt skyrocketed, and so did expenditures on our defense companies. Billionaires boomed!

But Ronnie was a hard man to replace. A decade went by without a true champion. Then we found George W. Bush. George is more than the great communicator Reagan was; he's truly one of us. We don't have to explain to him the benefits of coddling the rich and powerful—he's known them all his life. His billionaire friends helped him get places his brains couldn't, like Andover, Yale, and Harvard. We bailed out his failed business ventures and paid his way into politics.

George has done a bang-up job for us so far, laying things out just right for the long term: carefully appointing wealth-friendly judges to the bench, redrawing congressional districts to favor our boys, and even letting our companies count the votes at election time.

With Dubya in the pulpit, we don't even have to sing in the choir. And like Ronnie, he's got that down-home veneer. Democracy, baby—play the game! In fact, we may be just one presidency away from winning our long battle for hegemony. George is helping to ensure that America will always be a place where corporations come first, where no billionaire is left behind, and where social services are a freak of history.

Huzzah! ▪

You're either on the outside or the inside, and the only thing that can get you on the inside is money.

— JOE SCARBOROUGH
FORMER CONGRESSMAN (R-FL)

Congress

Club membership, with privileges

CHARMING NOTION, THAT MR. SMITH can trundle off to Washington and change the world, or that little Johnny or Jane Q. Public has any business dreaming of a place in the halls of power. Our bouncers are waiting at the doors of Congress, and *they are checking portfolios*. What does it take to open the golden ropes? Nothing more than a hell of a lot of gold.

Our club is getting more exclusive with every election. The freshman class of the 108th Congress (2002) has been the spiffiest yet. Of the 63 first-time members, 27 are millionaires, with fortunes in such lobby-friendly industries as banking, oil, and pharmaceuticals. That's a delicious 43 percent, up from 33 percent of new members in 2000. Since millionaires make up only 1 percent of the population, you can see just where that sappy bromide about government of, by, and for the people went.

The party's even better if we zero in on the Senate, mansion to at least 40 millionaires (22 Republicans, 18 Democrats). The CEO (official title: "majority leader"), Bill Frist (R-TN), runs a

Dick's Task Force

Nowhere was President Bush's devotion to corporate profits over public health more evident than in our dear friend Dick Cheney's secret Energy Policy Task Force. The vice president met with some of the nation's biggest polluters and their lobbyists to construct an energy policy that would reward Republican campaign contributors in the oil, coal, electric-utility and nuclear industries. The result of these closed-door meetings? Policies that

continued

hospital chain and is worth anywhere from $15 million to $42 million (love that fuzzy math).

Sure, we have our share of class traitors: that irksome, if loaded, liberal Jon Corzine (D-NJ), and the feckless John Kerry, marauding for things like universal health care. We've also got a smattering of lumpens—ten senators worth less than $100,000. They're a good alibi (keep dreaming, little Johnny), but do we really need all ten? Give us a cycle or two.

Some do-gooder, carping about the capture of politics by money, said that publicizing senators' wealth shows "the public the financial stake their elected officials have." And? Is there a problem here?

So how do we do it? As with everything else, we pay and pay and then play—with your money and lives. Votes can run up to $70 per for a congressional seat, but the largesse almost always pays off. In 2000, the top spenders in 85 percent of Senate races won; 94 percent of top spenders won in the House.

Where do we get the bread? Well, some of us spend buckets of our own, but mostly we keep the door wide open to our dear friends the lobbyists.

LOVING THOSE LOBBYISTS

If you prefer buying votes to casting them, if you don't have the time to serve private interests through "public service," then pick up a Beltway power suit, slap on those Bruno Maglis, and start clicking your heels in our House on the Hill or, better still, outside the Oval Office. You'll get your way long before poor Dorothy gets home to Kansas.

As far as the White House goes, chances are you'd be giving money to George W. Bush. Over the last six years, more than 1,300 registered lobbyists representing 6,000 clients have given more than $1.8 million to Dubya. Senator Kerry received a comparatively paltry $520,000 from 442 lobbyists representing 3,000 clients during the same period. (Combined, that's over half of all companies that hire registered lobbyists.)

Many of the lobbyists donating privately to Bush also raise serious coin for the president. No fewer than 550 are so-called bundlers, who rake in sums of $50,000 to $200,000 for the honor of nifty Lone Star names like Maverick, Pioneer, and Ranger. Fifty-two super-mega-lobbyists have raised more than $6 million for Bush. These fattest of cats represent companies that have paid them $146 million for lobbying since Bush took office—a mere pittance compared with the billion-dollar profits that patronage from on high can dole out!

Maybe some legislation comes with the titles, too? Smart money says yes. After all, Bush appointed 92 lobbyists to his transition's advisory teams in 2000 and 2001, many assigned to the very branches of government they had just spent millions to influence. One former Bush Pioneer, lobbyist John Schmitz, represented a health-care company that seemed

will hopefully open protected areas of the East and West coasts, the Arctic National Wildlife Refuge, and areas around Yellowstone Park to oil and gas drilling. Meanwhile, the task force resulted in the gutting of research into alternative energy sources and efficient energy use. Talk about maximizing your profit!

to hand-write into the recently passed Medicare Prescription Drug Bill a provision for making prescriptions and medical records available electronically—something Schmitz's company is expert in. *Voilà!*

K STREET GOES ELEPHANT ALLEY

You might think that lobbyists are equal-opportunity vultures who hedge their bets by giving equally to Republicans and Democrats. That was then, greenhorns, but with the saloon tilted Republican since 1994 and Sheriff Dubya in town, things have changed. Just ten years ago, corporate contributions from major sectors (energy, accounting, Big Pharma—all our favorite things) were almost evenly split between donkey and elephant. But now the Good Ole Boys' Party has a two-to-one advantage in corporate cash.

These miracles don't just happen. Since the 2000 election Rick Santorum, the Republican junior senator from Pennsylvania, has been holding weekly meetings with handpicked GOP lobbyists, GOP reps, and White House staff—Democrats and media *not* invited. These meetings address how to fill key positions in industry and the trade-association world with the "right" people. They're "right," all right: GOP House and Senate staffers, White House aides, and lobbyists with mad GOP cred. Every good Republican then rallies around these horses.

The operation has been highly successful, measured by legislation and policies that benefit the moneyed few at the expense of the hapless many. Dems have choked on the bitter fruit: two tax cuts that brazenly enrich the rich, the scuttling of environmental and workplace regulations, FCC rules giving the nod and wink to large media conglomerates. To the populist pieties thrown in our pretty faces, we say, "We're here, we don't care, get used to it!"

Some smart magazine hack, with a nose for our winning ways, remarked, "If today's GOP leaders put as much energy into shaping K Street as their predecessors did into selecting judges and executive-branch nominees, it's because lobbying jobs have become the foundation of a powerful new force in Washington politics: a Republican political machine. Like the urban Democratic machines of yore, this one is built upon patronage, contracts, and one-party rule."

But unlike legendary Chicago mayor Richard J. Daley, who rewarded party functionaries with jobs in the municipal bureaucracy, the GOP is building its machine outside government, among Washington's thousands of trade associations and corporate offices, their tens of thousands of employees, and the hundreds of millions of dollars in political money at their disposal. Whine on, crazies, we'll keep the diamonds.

— Merchant F. Arms / Jeremy Varon

FACTOID
Minimum number of federal lobbyists registered since 1999 whose interests cover "terror" or "security" issues: 444.

FACTOID
Percentage of federal discretionary spending in 2001 devoted to "homeland security" or the Department of Defense: 51.

*The only reason to have money is to tell any
SOB in the world to go to hell.*

— HUMPHREY BOGART

Double-U-Speak

Talking to the president

Do	Don't
SPEAK SLOWLY AND USE SMALL WORDS.	ASK HIM DIRECT QUESTIONS.
RESPOND CHEERFULLY TO YOUR NEW NICKNAME.	CALL HIM ANYTHING OTHER THAN "MR. PRESIDENT."
TALK ABOUT BROAD TOPICS, SUCH AS FREEDOM, DEMOCRACY, AND AMERICA.	TALK ABOUT SPECIFICS, SUCH AS CIVIL LIBERTIES, ELECTIONS, AND THE CONSTITUTION.
REMIND HIM THAT YOU'RE A "BIG DONOR."	OFFER HIM A BLANK CHECK.
MENTION HIS RANCH IN TEXAS.	MENTION ANY FOREIGN COUNTRIES OTHER THAN ENGLAND, FRANCE, OR CUBA.
PRAISE HIS SUCCESS ON NO CHILD LEFT BEHIND.	PRAISE HIS DAUGHTERS' CUTE BEHINDS.
MARVEL AT HOW MUCH FUN IT MUST HAVE BEEN TO RUN A BASEBALL TEAM.	ASK HIM HOW TAXPAYERS IN ARLINGTON, TEXAS, ARE ENJOYING THE STADIUM THEY BOUGHT HIM.
TELL THE JOKE ABOUT THE COMMUNIST, THE HIPPIE, AND THE TERRORIST.	TELL THE JOKE ABOUT THE FRAT BOY, THE OILMAN, AND THE RANDY ENGLISHMAN.
LAMENT THE DAMAGED REPUTATION OF BIG BUSINESS WROUGHT BY THE MISDEEDS OF A FEW.	ASK HIM HOW HE DODGED THE BULLET ON "THAT HARKEN BUSINESS."
ASK HIM TO "DROP BY FOR A VISIT ANYTIME."	ASK HIM TO "DROP BY AFTER KERRY'S INAUGURATION."

Talking about the president

Don't	Do
USE TERMS LIKE "PUPPET" AND "HIRED GUN."	SUBTLY REMARK TO HIS STAFF HOW EXPENSIVE ELECTIONS ARE THESE DAYS.
MENTION HOW MUCH MORE MONEY YOU'VE MADE AS A RESULT OF HIS CORPORATE-ASSISTANCE POLICIES.	REMIND HIS PEOPLE WHO IS FUNDING THE GOVERNMENT'S DEFICIT SPENDING.
SAY, "LET'S GET ALL 'HOMELAND SECURITY' ON SICK PEOPLE TRYING TO BUY DRUGS FROM CANADA."	SAY, "LET'S SHOW SICK AMERICANS WE CARE BY GIVING THEM ACCESS TO ONLY THE 'GOLD STANDARD' OF DRUGS."

Talking about the president to the public

Don't	Do
TALK ABOUT HOW EASY AND PROFITABLE NO-BID DEFENSE CONTRACTS ARE.	SAY, "OUR YOUNG SOLDIERS DESERVE THE BEST."
THANK HIM FOR ENABLING THE CONCENTRATION OF MASS MEDIA INTO A UNIFORM, CONSERVATIVE MESSAGE.	THANK HIM FOR ELIMINATING THE CONFUSION WHEN SO MANY PEOPLE ARE TRYING TO TELL US SO MANY DIFFERENT THINGS.
PRAISE HIM FOR EASING RESTRAINTS ON HAZARDOUS AIR EMISSIONS AND IGNORING THAT GLOBAL-WARMING HOAX.	PRAISE HIM FOR HIS EFFORTS TO MAKE MARS HABITABLE FOR FUTURE GENERATIONS OF AMERICANS.

— Thurston Howell IV/Kurt Opprecht

George W. Bush Owner's Manual

Congratulations on your purchase of "Dubya," the President of the United States, 2000-2004 model.* This release incorporates significant improvements on the earlier Bush model (1988-1992).

- Simpler vocabulary / worldview
- Increased pugnaciousness
- Fewer scruples
- More self-righteousness
- Less sensitivity to public opinion
- Greater bellicosity
- More fun to have beer with
- Special smokescreen capability
- Advanced programmability
- Does not require reading of lips
- Does remove Saddam
- Does not speak French

INSTALLATION
If an electoral victory does not work, this should be taken care of by the Supreme Court and / or next-of-kin governors.

TURNING YOUR PRESIDENT ON
Should the enclosed puppy, baseball game, apple pie, charming sorority wife, or pretzel stick fail to start the President, try any of the

*Dick Cheney (purchased separately) required for operation.

❝ There's an old saying in Tennessee—I know it's in Texas, probably in Tennessee—that says, fool me once, shame on you. You fool me, you can't get fooled again. ❞

— George W. Bush
Nashville, September 17, 2002

❝ Sometimes, Washington is one of these towns where the person, people who think they've got the sharp elbow is the most effective person. ❞

— George W. Bush
New Orleans, December 4, 2002

following: NASCAR, horses, the American flag, a freshly cut check.

TURNING YOUR PRESIDENT OFF

Any of the following: political debate, compound sentences, nuanced arguments, polling places.

LIST OF FEATURES

Significantly **lowers** taxes for corporate and upper-income brackets.

Declares wars (requires three weeks' notice) and instigates smaller miscellaneous conflicts.

Shifts tax burden from unearned to earned income.

Nominates at least one reactionary Supreme Court justice.

Passes legislation as delivered.

Slices, dices, and **squelches** information.

Cuts vital social programs and education funding.

Removes environmental and worker-protection regulations.

Alienates nearly all historical allies.

Raises buckets (in some cases, oodles) of money.

Supplies one to 1,000 vetoes.

Converts budget surpluses into record-setting deficits.

Enriches the oil, pharmaceutical, health care, insurance, defense, and banking industries.

Provides corporate access to previously protected public lands.

Polarizes public opinion.

ACTION-FIGURE FUNCTIONS

Fighter pilot

Accessories: aircraft carrier, flight suit, codpiece (not included).

Cowboy

Accessories: horse, cowboy hat, boots, jeans; wistful, determined look in eye (included).

Vacation mode

Indicated by: proximity to Texas or Maine. (Note: will revert to vacation mode if left alone for more than one day.)

Absolute-power mode

Indicated by: wild declarations, increased use of hand gestures and terms "evil," "evildoers," "axis of evil," and "freedom."

Tax-cutting mode

Indicated by: creased brow, lowered eyelid, and clenched jaw, broken intermittently by nod and wink to rich friends. Found most often during campaign stops and fundraisers, usually in conjunction with unsubstantiated promises of job growth.

Compassionate-conservative mode

Indicated by: cute and lovable "Golly gee, I'm doing the best I can" disposition. (Closely resembles *Mad* magazine's Alfred E. Newman.)

Indignant self-righteous mode

Indicated by: threats, references to sacrifice, heroism, God, and bravery; generally followed by invasion of sovereign nation.

Cowboy mode

Indicated by: chip on shoulder, increase in swagger and bravado ("Bring 'em on!"). Also can be followed by invasion of sovereign nation.

Ugly American mode
Indicated by: indifference to United Nations, heightened contempt for non-English-speaking world.

Sleep mode
Distinguished from "meeting mode" only by the fact that eyes remain closed for more than ten minutes.

Frat-boy mode
(This mode has been discontinued.)

REMOTE OPERATION
Can be operated remotely from bunker or other undisclosed location. (This model not meant to operate autonomously.)

TROUBLESHOOTING
Should any of the following occur, immediately contact Karl Rove at the 24-hour Radical Support Hotline:

- Lands on aircraft carrier

- Declares end of hostilities in middle of a war

- Appears in public without prepared text

- Squanders sympathy of entire world within two years of vicious terrorist attack

This is a profit-motivated President. In the event of prolonged inaction, fill with campaign contributions (coin slot located in rear).

PROPER CARE OF YOUR PRESIDENT
DO NOT expose to network news outlets (other than Fox).

SHIELD your President from: the media (unless extensively coached and supervised), bright light, facts, press conferences, demonstrations, sudden changes in cultural climate.

AVOID all contact with: books (except westerns, picture

books, and comics), middle classes (except during campaign appearances).

AT ALL COST, KEEP AWAY FROM the following abstract concepts: civil liberties, self-determination, multilateralism.

FEEDING
Strictly American food.

ACCESSORIES TO YOUR PRESIDENT
- Flacks, yes men, neocons
- Miniature VHF aural-canal receiver chip, tuned to Karl Rove's matching transmitter
- Segway scooter (discontinued)
- Ranch
- One wife
- Two daughters
- Chain saw

MANUFACTURER'S NOTE
Look for these other fine presidential products in this series:

- Ronald Reagan Dogmatizer and Original Nonstick Fryer
- Herbert Hoover Wealth Concentrator and Juicer
- Richard Nixon Polarizer and Paranoia Ionizer
- Warren Harding Prohibition Profiteer and Martini Shaker ⚏

WARRANTY
With proper care, your President will, during a four-year term, fulfill the previously specified actions and duties. This warranty is completely null and void in event of the following:

- Weapons of mass destruction never materialize in his lifetime.

- Electoral College is eliminated.

- Ralph Nader drops out of race.

- Dick Cheney dies of heart attack or lack of soul.

- The polar ice caps melt.

Souvenirs from Your Sleepover

What to steal from the Lincoln Bedroom

FROSTED GLOBES: They go perfectly with the chair-leg lam

FINIALS: Much better on your chifforobe than here, no?

How boring. Don't bother.

POSTCARDS? Impress your friends with "authentic" cards cut from pictures. Don't forget to have them sent from the White House mailroom.

CHAIR LEGS: Make fun lamp bases for your guest powder room. Take two for a matched set!

TASSELS:
A very special item. [Th]ere's only two, so [be]tter take them both—[it's] less noticeable.

WHILE YOU'RE AT IT:
Who's sleeping next door?

ABE'S LACE BED CURTAINS:
The perfect historical touch for your little girl's wedding veil.

THE CREME DE LA CREME:
A piece of the action from dear old Abe.

— Claus von Bullion / Christopher Lione

4 Tips on How to Pull It Off

OK. You made your contribution to George's campaign and he invites you to spend a night in the Lincoln Bedroom. Enjoy—you deserve it. And if you want a souvenir, here's some practical advice.

1. BE PREPARED. Keep your implements small and dispose of them before you leave.

2. DON'T BE GREEDY. Just take a thing or two; leave something for the rest of us.

3. TIP THE HOUSE-KEEPER. She has lots of explaining to do after you've left.

4. TIP THE GUARD HANDSOMELY. He's less likely to check your bags while you're checking out.

The George W. Bush Presidential Library, Resort, and Casino

Announcing ...

. . . an extraordinary opportunity to invest in the nation's history and honor the presidency of George W. Bush.

SHARES

A public offering of shares in *The George W. Bush Presidential Library, Resort, and Casino Inc.*, a Liberian corporation, will take place in November 2004. Shares may be purchased from selected brokers in million-dollar lots.

The George W. Bush Presidential Library, Resort, and Casino will represent the ultimate in information-technology and gaming facilities. The first offshore presidential library, the complex will be sited on the Tax Shelter Island of Tricky Cayman in the Lesser Antilles.

Investments will not only yield handsome offshore revenues and a handsome tax write-off but will provide valuable Caribbean real estate with year-round docking rights for yachts and other pleasure craft, not to mention the opportunity to express continuing gratitude to the president for the ongoing policies and legacies of his groundbreaking administration.

THE LIBRARY

In addition to the president's scholarly papers, philosophical treatises, Texas prisoners' death sentences, and risqué doodles from UN briefings, the Bush Library will include the president's private collection of sports memorabilia and the Bush Archives.

Once inside, unescorted visitors enter the National Security Lounge for a full body-cavity search. On the right and left walls will be located the Hall of Fame, where are prominently displayed the names and logos of individuals or corporations that have contributed or bundled more than $5 million to Bush election campaigns.

After climbing the sweeping staircase of travertine marble with onyx-and-inlaid-silver railings, the visitor enters Energy Hall (a gift of the Mobil-Exxon Foundation).

Included in the first exhibition: The empty Jack Daniels bottle from which Mr. Bush had his last drink; a pair of Adidas running shoes, bronzed; the drool-stained pillow on which Mr. Bush slept during the 2000 campaign; the original daily brief regarding Osama bin Laden's intention to attack the US; the book the president was reading to school-children when notified of the attack on the World Trade Center; the Nautilus machine on which he deeply contemplated declaring war on Iraq; a gift box of halvah; Saddam Hussein's dental X-rays; and a single pretzel preserved in

Billionaire's Jeopardy

Potable Polo Ponies	It Rhymes with SchmENRON	Trophy Wives & Prenups	Zillions	Dubious Charities	"You're the MAN!"
$1 MIL	$1 MIL	$1 MIL	$1 MIL	$1 MIL	$1 MIL
$2 MIL	$2 MIL	$2 MIL	$2 MIL	$2 MIL	$2 MIL
$3 MIL	$3 MIL	$3 MIL	$3 MIL	$3 MIL	$3 MIL
$4 MIL	$4 MIL	$4 MIL	$4 MIL	$4 MIL	$4 MIL
$5 MIL	$5 MIL	$5 MIL	$5 MIL	$5 MIL	$5 MIL

formaldehyde. Note the backlit portrait of VP Dick Cheney, whose eyes follow you around the room.

THE BUSH ARCHIVES (TOP-SECRET CLEARANCE REQUIRED)
All the president's personal state papers and National Guard records will be stored in a polished spheroid time capsule of hardened titanium steel, set to remain hermetically sealed until the year 2104.

THE CONFERENCE CENTER AND RESORT
Sited on the remote, beautiful Tax Shelter Island, this facility will include a five-star hotel with gourmet restaurants, a world-class spa, state-of-the-art swimming pools, a

professional polo field, three tournament-caliber golf courses, all-weather tennis courts, miles of pristine sandy beaches, and the Oil, Gas, and Coal Companies Auditorium.

BUSHWORLD

For kids, BushWorld™ Theme Park on nearby Tax Shelter Cay will offer educational Family Fun™! Rides and exhibits will include Afghan-Land, where you'll pursue Osama bin Laden on a madcap chase through rugged mountains and rocky valleys amid the fragrance of opium poppies, avoiding fanatical Taliban shooters. Among the concessions will be the famous Hard Right Café.

Wholesome family entertainment will be presented at the BarbaraJenna Auditorium. Shows twice daily will feature the best Christian rock groups and the US Army Reserve Band.

CONFERENCE FACILITIES

The Dick Cheney Secret Meeting Center will be available for corporate-planning groups of all sizes. It is a handsome, detached structure, with an auditorium swept daily for listening devices and capable of seating 1,000. Sensitive documents can be shredded in the Off the Record Room.

FACTOID

For George W. Bush's future presidential library, the Saudi ambassador has given him a painting valued at $1 million.

FACTOID

According to Forbes, the chance that a billionaire in America is self-made is 1:1.

FACTOID

Chance that a network television advertisement is paid for by one of the 100 largest US corporations: 3 in 4.

FACTOID

Factor by which Americans' total debt to private lenders for college tuition has increased since 1995: 4.

GAMING FACILITIES

For the risk takers among our guests, there will be the Fulgencio Batista Memorial Casino, filled with vintage gaming tables, formerly of Havana's Hotel Nacional (many with the sweat of erstwhile pit boss Jake Lansky still on them). The room will be decorated in its original 1950s Art Deco style, honoring the former Cuban president for his role in giving George H.W. Bush his start in international relations.

SECURITY

• The island will be accessible only by private yacht, corporate jet, and Trident-class submarine.

• Professional soldiers from G-Eye Joe (a subsidiary of Halliburton) will patrol the grounds around the clock.

• The surrounding coast will be guarded by the Qwackenhut Navy.

• Employee security will be handled by a Republican Guard interrogation team recently engaged by CACI International following the success of their training films for the troops at Abu Ghraib prison.

• The resort's outer walls will be capable of withstanding a low-yield nuclear blast.

The George W. Bush Presidential Library, Resort, and Casino, Inc., in keeping with the policy of the Bush administration, does not warrant the truth of any statement in this offering circular.

— Kent Scarsdale IV / Richard Lingeman

Hacking an Election

Hint: build the machines yourself

NOTHING'S BETTER THAN A contested election to prove who's got the muscle in a republic; we easily won the shoving match of 2000. But no sooner had our fave legal firm (Rehnquist, Scalia, Thomas, O'Connor & Kennedy, LLP) appointed Dubya our supreme commander than the middle-class pundits cried foul, blaming everything from "hanging chads" and "butterfly ballots" to obsolete voting machines. Sore losers? Perhaps. But there's a lesson to be learned: upgrading our electoral system is in order.

Why upgrade? Well, not only is there a much handier way to put our thumb on the scale, but there's money to be made from owning the scale as well. As a result of the brouhaha in Florida, Congress passed the Help America Vote Act, which allocated $3.9 billion for upgrading to sparkling new electronic voting systems. Need we say more?

In the November 2004 election, about 50 million citizens will vote using paperless

FACTOID

In the 2004 elections, 29 percent of US voters will have cast their vote via a computer system producing no paper record.

touch-screen voting machines, while 55 million more will rely on optical ballot-scan machines.

Investment opportunities are wide-reaching and varied, and ultimately not limited to the US. A prime example of how to take advantage of the opportunities in the voting-machine industry is provided by Walden O'Dell, chief executive of ATM maker Diebold. His touch-screen voting machines are used in dozens of states and districts across the US. O'Dell is a productive fundraiser for Republican causes who wrote in a letter to Bush supporters in 2003: "I am committed to helping Ohio deliver its electoral votes to the president next year."

COMPLIANT TECHNOLOGY
(NO NEED TO PAY OFF A MACHINE, RIGHT?)

These e-voting machines are faster and simpler to use than paper ballots or those ancient mechanical contraptions. And best of all, they have the potential to make fixing an election a breeze.

The machines are said to be easy to "hack"—merely tinker with the source code, and they'll spit out whatever you wish. The government is under pressure to step in and require e-voting machine makers to provide printed-paper receipts. But so far so good. (Hey, the last place we want the government sticking its nose is free elections, right?) As usual, we have friends on the inside. Chuck Hagel, GOP senator from Nebraska, is a former chairman of electronic-voting machine company ES&S, and still maintains financial ties to the company.

Truth be told, these machines have already helped us win elections we might have lost, although we're still getting the bugs out (so to speak):

• ES&S manufactured the only voting machines used in Nebraska for Hagel's election campaigns in both 1996 and 2002. A first-time candidate in 1996 who had lived out of state for two decades, Hagel somehow managed to come from behind to win two major upsets: first in

FACTOID

Eighty-three percent of the itemized campaign contributions for the 2002 elections was given by less than one tenth of 1 percent of the US population.

FACTOID

In the 2002 midterm races, House and Senate incumbents raised $571 million for their reelection campaigns; challengers raised a paltry $168 million. Ninety-eight percent of House incumbents, and 85 percent of incumbent senators, were reelected.

FACTOID

In nine out of ten cases, a 2002 congressional race was won by the candidate whose campaign spent the most.

the Republican primary, then against Democrat Ben Nelson, a popular former governor. Nelson started the campaign with a 65 to 18 percent lead in the polls, but Hagel still collected 56 percent of the vote, becoming the state's first Republican senator in 24 years.

• After two Republican candidates for commissioner in Scurry County, Texas, won in a landslide in 2002, liberal-leaning poll workers became suspicious. They had a new computer chip flown in and also counted ballots by hand. Alas, in the end they discovered that Democrats had won the election handily, and overturned the result.

• During the 2000 presidential election in Florida, the tabulation system for Volusia County's optical-scan system subtracted votes from Al Gore. In a precinct where a mere 412 people voted, Gore's tally equaled *negative* 16,022 votes, while the Bush-Cheney ticket was credited with 2,813 votes. Lucky for us, the attention of the media was focused elsewhere, or, like Lucy Ricardo, we might have had some 'splainin' to do.

• In 2000 in Allamakee County, Iowa, 300 ballots fed into an optical-scan machine produced four million votes. "We don't have four million voters in the state of Iowa," claimed County Auditor Bill Roe Jr. Not bad. Once again, right idea, just not subtle enough.

— Chase D. Gold / Adam Penenberg

Rovespeak Lexicon

A handy reference for correlating White House spin with actual policy

ECONOMIC POLICY

Death tax: For generations, one of the few things keeping us from establishing a nobility without *noblesse oblige* in this country has been the estate tax. By recasting this as the "death tax," we have been able to capitalize on the most sentimental instincts of working taxpayers.

Give industry a say: The business of America is business, and nobody knows business like business, so nobody knows how the country should be run like business! Some of you may remember this policy's first iteration, when we called it "Reaganomics."

Economic recovery: This administration's policies have done wonders for the economy of India by shipping America's extra jobs to Bangalore.

ENVIRONMENTAL POLICY

Healthy Forests Initiative: Formerly: "logging." This is our most effective spin yet. Thank God and Henry Ford that no one in the public actually

"My accountant validates me."

reads beyond the titles of legislation. Just remember, keep pushing the idea that Healthy Forests is *good for the environment*—after all, no trees, no California wildfires.

Clear Skies Act: Environmental regulations getting you down? The solution is the Clear Skies Act, an initiative to keep America's skies clear ... clear for profit, that is. Why bother to outfit that power plant with expensive scrubbers? It's not like *your* kids have to live downwind of it!

Climate enhancement: As we can deny global warming for only so long, we've decided that the administration's second term will put a positive spin on matters by referring to rising sea levels, sweltering summers, global catastrophes, etc., as "climate enhancement." Our market analysts indicate that this policy will open up great opportunities in real-estate investment.

FOREIGN AFFAIRS

Operation Iraqi Freedom: Dick C.'s original name for this plan was Operation Iraqi Free Oil, but Karl didn't think that would go over so well in the press. Stand by for Operation San Francisco Freedom and Operation Greenwich Village Freedom.

Homeland security: Our new border-control-cum-immigration policy, designed to keep terrorists out, but allow low-wage workers in. As we all know, the best aliens are those who work for less than minimum wage.

Enemy combatant: If you're not with us, you're against us! By classifying someone as an "enemy combatant," we effectively revoke their citizenship and avoid that pesky Bill of Rights. Future enemy combatants: swarthy foreigners, Michael Moore, Florida democrats.

— Rob D. Tillman / Ken Mondschein

Your horse farm 30 miles inland from Kennebunkport can be tropical beach-front property in five or six years. Imagine the added value of your Aspen getaway if it can also be marketed as a desert paradise—and within the same season!

Billionocracy

Our agenda for the future

BILLIONAIRES FOR BUSH IS NOT JUST about short-term handouts to corporations; we're about maintaining a billionaire-friendly America, forever. What will our billionocracy look like? Here are some rough outlines.

Allow corporations to run for office. Eliminate the present clumsy policy of having a mere representative of Enron in the presidency, or of Halliburton in the vice presidency, or of Big Pharma in Congress. Direct participation is much more efficient. (And think of the advertising potential: "The AstraZeneca Speaker of the House"!)

Pay appointed officials and public servants in stock options. Just like our CEOs, public servants from the White House to the EPA need the right incentive structures. Flat salaries, doled out from the public purse, are regressive and counterproductive. Compensation tied exclusively to the relevant sector's stock value is the answer. A mix of defense, oil, and construction companies for State Department officials; heavy-industry companies for EPA employees; Big Pharma for the Department of Health.

George W.'s tax cuts gave $50,000-plus to everyone making over $1 million, and just $350 each to 80 percent of America's families. By 2010 the benefits will increase to $85,000 for the richest among us, and disappear for some of the less wealthy. George has managed to keep the masses content with their paltry returns, while we get permanent cuts in five figures.

Eliminate corporate liability. America's corporations are uniquely suited to determine which safety precautions are necessary and affordable. Activist judges must not be allowed to trump our decisions.

Scrap all social programs. Who needs Social Security, public education, and free health care? We certainly didn't. Rather than slowly starve these programs of funds with more wars and more tax cuts, isn't it more merciful to pull the plug now?

One dollar, one vote. Forget the fiddly campaign-finance law, and forget the Electoral College. To truly ensure that America has a political system that answers to wealth, each person will get a number of votes equivalent to his net worth. Those in debt will receive negative votes.

War on economic terror at home. While our attention is drawn abroad, workers under our very noses are terrorizing patriotic companies by union organizing, calling for legislation to raise the minimum wage, and striking for health coverage. Their demands threaten the Constitution's guarantee of free markets and private property. They amount to nothing less than treason in this time of war.

Privatize war. Halliburton provides bases, supplies, food, vehicles, weaponry, and ammunition to the army and has its own private security company to guard its installations. Why is the US still maintaining a public-sector military? Privatization would insulate the administration from criticism and scrutiny, and allow Halliburton to subcontract cheaper non-American combatants to absorb casualties. The

British Empire was built on the strength of private corporations conquering territory for commercial gain; America should follow this example.

Expand the prison-industrial labor force. Prisoners are the ideal workforce. They cannot demand raises or benefits, organize labor unions, or leave to find a better job. We would grow this invaluable pool of labor by expanding the war on nonviolent drug users and by toughening mandatory minimum sentences. This promises to be even more effective than President Bush's current plan to import and export immigrant labor according to the needs of corporate America.

Introduce efficiency tracking for public schools. Rather than waste resources educating every child, we must recognize that most will end up in service jobs. Billionaires would help the government develop an early tracking program to mark these Potential Low-Wage Earners (PLOWs) at the age of 5 and save them the trouble, and us the cost, of a formal education.

Corporate sponsorship of college students. Replace what's left of federal financial-aid programs with corporate sponsorship. We fund students' degrees, and in return they give us ten years' indentured servitude.

Move the EPA inside the Chamber of Commerce. Economic growth and environmental sustainability are perfectly compatible, but only commercial experts can properly identify the ripe opportunities for exploitation.

Increase oil and coal subsidies. We cannot afford to move toward energy efficiency or alternatives that would make America less vulnerable militarily, economically, and environmentally. There's no money in that kind of stability. Boosting subsidies to our big energy companies is the best way of maintaining the status quo (and making a bit more money on the side).

Repeal unjust ban on international bribery. The current Foreign Corrupt Practices Act prevents us from bribing foreign officials. Since we bribe our own officials, it is unjust not to offer the same courtesy to officials from poorer countries. Halliburton has blazed a trail in, we're told, giving $180 million in bribes to Nigerian officials. We should transform that act of civil disobedience into a full-fledged campaign to overturn this unjust law. ∎

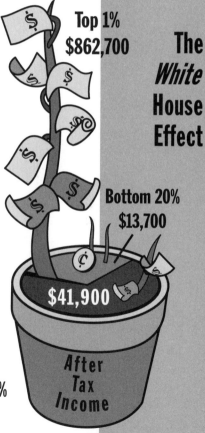

Top 1%
$862,700

The
White
House
Effect

Bottom 20%
$13,700

$41,900

Middle 20%

After
Tax
Income

The days of looking the other way while despotic regimes
trample human rights, rob their nation's wealth,
and then excuse their failings by feeding their people a
steady diet of anti-Western hatred are over.

— DICK CHENEY
FEBRUARY 6, 2004

Making Billions from Your Government Position

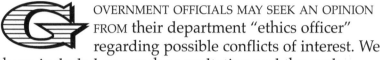

A legal opinion

OVERNMENT OFFICIALS MAY SEEK AN OPINION FROM their department "ethics officer" regarding possible conflicts of interest. We have included one such consultation and the reply.

From: Office of the White House Counsel
1600 Pennsylvania Avenue
Washington, D.C. 20010

To: Office of Clandestine Ethics
Street address: Undisclosed
Washington, D.C. Zip code: Classified

Dear Sir(s):

Because current Conflict of Interest (COI) law requires the approval of counsel to allow government officials to profit from their positions, we ask you at the Office of Clandestine Ethics (OCE) to help legitimize COI waivers to each of the below individuals. Your cooperation will be remembered at Christmastime.

Sincerely,
[name withheld pending judicial appointment]

THE RESULTING OPINIONS:

1. Vice President Richard Cheney is Washington's foremost contractor/statesman. Cheney receives "deferred" payments annually between $100,000 and $1 million from Halliburton, from which he "resigned" upon assuming the vice presidency.

Dear Mr. Counsel:
Seeing as Halliburton is the chief recipient of Pentagon contracts emanating from Iraq, it would be boorish to question why or how such arrangement came about. As for Cheney's possible receipt of funds earned as a direct result of his role in ordering the Iraq invasion, he is hereby exempt from federal Conflict of Interest law.

2. Through his father, President George W. Bush is associated with a private equity firm that owns companies which contract with the Department of Defense and three of its four highest-grossing missile-defense contractors: Boeing, Raytheon, and Northrop Grumman. President Bush has left Pyongyang's fissile material unattended, issued childish insults about North Korea's leader, and threatened to invade. Subsequently, the president authorized his subordinates to increase outlays to Raytheon, Boeing, and Northrop Grumman to defend the United States against North Korea. We are concerned that these actions may be construed as a conflict of interest.

Dear Sir:
In accordance with accepted ethics practices, we recommend that the president does not accept a poodle or fur coat from Boeing, Northrop, or Raytheon. Of course, even if Mr. Bush's wife were a managing partner in Carlyle, the firm to which it is presumed that you refer, it wouldn't matter. Presidents are exempt from COI laws.

3. Between stints at the Pentagon and its corporate partners, Donald Rumsfeld directed a study for the congressman from Lockheed-Martin's district in Marietta, Georgia—Newt Gingrich. He urged Congress to rearm America with high-tech weapons that Lockheed itself was slated to develop.

Sir:
The OCE declares Rumsfeld above suspicion and beyond contempt.

4. As chairman of the Defense Policy Board (the DoD advisory group), Richard Perle has performed exemplary work in acquiring for his firm a $20 million consulting contract from Boeing. We feel this is not just a good idea, it's above the law. Could you confirm?

Hi Guy,
You bet we can. Of the Defense Policy Board's 30 members, nine are or have been associated with companies that accumulated more than $76 billion in defense contracts in 2001 and 2002, and we officially waive conflict restrictions against all of them. We like people associated with billions of dollars.

5. Transportation Secretary Norman Mineta, Veterans Affairs Secretary Anthony Principi, and wife of the vice president Lynne Cheney have each held positions at Lockheed. To some, this doesn't look good.

Hey Big Guy,
Lockheed didn't get to be the Pentagon's biggest contractor for nothing.

6. Douglas Feith, the undersecretary of defense for policy, is the third-ranking civilian in the Pentagon. Feith founded International Advisors Inc., a lobbying firm, and hired Perle in 1989. Perle got him his current job.

Dude,
Douglas Feith is no way conflicted about his role in acquiring business for his associates. We at the OCE have taken the liberty of nominating him for the U.S. Chamber of Commerce's Contractor of the Year Award.

7. Rep. Curt Weldon, who sponsored legislation behind the Lockheed/Gingrich study, and Feith were colleagues on the contractor-financed missile-defense lobby group Center for Strategic Policy.

Comrade,
We relieve the Honorable Mr. Weldon of responsibility for any actions he has taken that may have deleterious effects on the health and welfare of his constituents through the use of their tax dollars.

8. Feith's law firm, Feith and Zell, represented defense-industry clients, including Northrop Grumman and Loral Space & Communications.

Amigo,
We are impressed by Feith's tireless work ethic.

9. Deputy Secretary of Defense Paul Wolfowitz, Pentagon Comptroller Dov Zakheim, Vice Presidential Chief of Staff I. Lewis Libby, and NASA Administrator (and prospective successor to Rumsfeld) Sean O'Keefe all had consulting contracts or served as paid advisory-board members for Northrop Grumman prior to joining the administration.

Mah Brother,
We at the OCE are pooling our 401(K) funds to purchase shares in Northrop.
— **Matt Reiss**

FICTION

Buying an Invasion

DARKENED ENTRANCE ON THE ALLEY SIDE OF A well-known Washington, DC, cigar bar on K Street. A dark figure in a blue pin-striped suit, heels clicking against the high-rent cobblestone alleyway, passes a dumpster and approaches the delivery entrance.

On the far side of the dumpster a happy wino is deep-throating a bottle of the good stuff. The man in the suit lowers his eyes, pushes open the double doors, and disappears inside with only the eerie glow of a single dim bulb glinting off his American-flag pin.

A long black limo crawls slowly down that same alley just a moment later. Two men jump out, spinning around in SWAT-like formation, guns aquiver, silencers attached.

The wino belts out the words to an obscure love song, "I love you more every day," and a three-pieced commando unloads a quiet *poof* into his skull. The sound of breaking glass shatters the silence of the alleyway.

A heavy, lumbering figure in a gray flannel suit exits the rear seat of the limo, dusts off his lapel, and, hunched forward, walks heavily toward the door held open by his contractors.

Inside, the cigar smoke is thick, and the furniture plush. The room is almost completely dark. A waiter opens a fresh box of Habanos, cuts, and offers one to each of the two men.

The waiter flicks the lighter and puts it to the vice president's cigar. Dick sucks hard. The red glow lights gleam off the chestnut tabletop to reveal the face of Fidel Castro's nephew, the congressman from Miami.

"It's a big step from congressman to president, young man."

"Do you think I'm not prepared for it, Mr. Vice President?"

"I suppose it doesn't matter. If you fail, you fail."

"We are prepared, I assure you."

"Have you got the money?"

"The down payment? My man did the wire transfer himself. Your man at Halliburton confirmed it this afternoon. The Cayman subsidiary."

"Fine. You don't mind if I confirm that myself before we mobilize the 101st?"

"I would expect nothing less, Mr. Vice President."

"I understand a fleet of construction barges arrived on the Dominican coast this evening. Have you secured enough contractors to complete the construction project on schedule?"

"Mr. Vice President, mark my words, there will be a shiny new Disneyland in Revolution Square in time for your first inauguration parade."

"Say hello to your uncle for me."   — Matt Reiss

Judicious Investing

Court jesting for pros

YOU KNOW AS SURE AS DEATH AND diamonds that at some point some pesky peon is going to sue you. You know lots of ways your cash can protect you, from the high-priced firms you hire to the settlements you pay. But so many of us overlook a critical tactic: we can buy judges.

Is "buy" too crass a word? Sure, it's done, but outright purchase is really a tactic of the petit bourgeoisie. The more appropriate term, perhaps, is "invest"—through judicious contributions to judges' election campaigns. Then, when one of "your" judges hears your case, you'll get a friendly ear.

Thirty-three states elect their Supreme Court justices and some or all of their other judges. Indirect though it may be, the approach works. One Pennsylvania lobbyist proudly notes that his group's contributions pay for a pro-business bias on the bench. About his philosophy, he notes that "the idea is a George Meany quote, 'It's a whole lot easier to elect people who think like you than it is to educate them once they've been elected.' That is our motto and that is what we go by." Nationally, lawyers and business

A 1938 law— damn that New Deal!—meant that 90 million workers have a right to time-and-a-half pay for overtime. Worse, we have to shell out $2 billion worth of litigation each year, quibbling over entitlements when we try to take them away illegally. Bush changed the law so that eight million middle-income workers, including nurses, lost their right to overtime pay. He cleverly inserted a provision increasing the number of low-income workers covered by the overtime law so he could claim he was fighting for the little guy.

interests contribute the most. Don't worry about unpleasant publicity; little attention is given to judicial races, so you can contribute and keep a low profile!

Big contributors think the cash is a good investment: three quarters of Texas lawyers, who make the vast majority of judicial-election contributions in that state, think the contributions have "significant" influence on outcomes. One study characterizes the level of cash given by lawyers to Texas judges as putting judges on retainer.

However much a judge doth protest that his decision is unaffected by the cash, we know better. Even U.S. Supreme Court Justices Kennedy and Breyer have taken note of how effective our "contributions to justice" appear to be. Other judges also acknowledge the correlation. Nearly half of Texas judges think the contributions affect outcomes.

Anecdotal reports suggest the cash works. (As if we had any doubt!) And studies have given broader empirical underpinnings to this perception.

North Carolina barely hides the connection between contributions and outcomes: "Responding to a protest from trial judges over recent changes in [North Carolina's] judicial conduct rules," their Supreme Court has sent every state judge a memo defending the changes that "allow candidates to directly ask lawyers and others for campaign contributions and dropped a prohibition against promising voters to rule certain ways if elected." Now we're talking! Unfortunately, the secret is out and the bidding wars have begun. Start investing now!   — Anastasia Romanov / Abigail Caplovitz

How Do We Love Thee, George?

Eight reasons why Dubya's the best investment we ever made

1. **Money, money, and money!** Bush's tax cuts mean trillions for us and tidbits for everyone else. Better still, they've left Americans with a crippling debt that their children will be paying back to us for years to come while the government slashes Social Security, education, and health care to avoid going bankrupt.

2. **We're making a killing in health care.** The health of Americans is important to us. In fact, it's worth about $1.6 trillion a year. Over the first three years of the Bush presidency, our drug companies averaged a 17 percent profit.

3. **The war chest.** Most presidents keep our defense contractors happy, but George is special. He's increased the defense budget, turned over lucrative government services to our companies, and topped it all off by destroying Iraq with our most expensive bombs—and then paying us to rebuild it. So while America gets more wars, and less money

George gave us a scare when he campaigned in 2000 with a promise to scrap outdated Cold War weapons programs. We stood to lose over $68 billion in lucrative (if useless) defense contracts. But that just turned out to be campaign talk, and thankfully Bush has kept all our programs and increased the defense budget by $90 billion. We knew we had nothing to worry about, since both George W. and George Sr. have been employees of the Carlyle Group (see page 82). Dubya then kindly looked the other way while we failed to pay $3 billion in taxes.

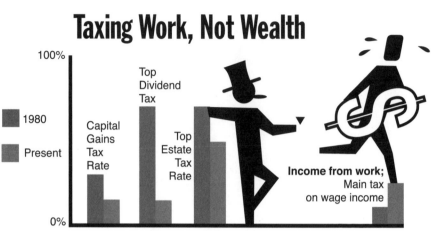

Taxing Work, Not Wealth

100%

1980

Present

Capital
Gains
Tax
Rate

Top
Dividend
Tax

Top
Estate
Tax
Rate

Income from work;
Main tax
on wage income

0%

We Americans with investment income and large amounts of inherited wealth
have recived a multitude of well-deserved tax breaks in recent years. Since
1980, the capital gains tax rate has dropped, the top dividend tax rate has
dropped, and the top estate tax rate on multimillionaires and billionaires has
dropped, with more cuts on the way! (It's been a different story for the middle
classes. Since 1980, the main tax on wage income, the payroll tax, has gone
up 25%.)

---

for social programs, families, and the future, we get $250
billion!

4. **Da juice.** George is an oilman, Dick is an oilman. We're
all oilmen! From Kyoto to Iraq, Bush has ensured that
whether it's global warming or global peace, our profits
come first. He even let us write his new energy bill and
give ourselves $30 billion in new subsidies.

5. **An hour is an hour is an hour.** Paying our workers
salaries is a necessary evil. But paying them overtime?
It may keep millions of families afloat, but it sure costs us

a lot of money. George fought the whining public and Congress to remove eight million workers' right to overtime pay, potentially saving us $1.9 billion a year, forever.

6. **Big media, big profits.** George knows the value of having media that'll make him look good, and we know the value of controlling what you think (and of making billions doing it). Again, George stood alone against a public outcry, a bipartisan Congress, and the foundations of America's democracy to ensure that our mega-media corporations can get even bigger.

7. **Department of Sticks and Berries.** Once, governments fought to protect your health and preserve the environment for your children. Maybe they just didn't appreciate how much money could be made. But George does. He's undone decades of terrible anti-wealth policies and fought hard for our right to make billions polluting the air, endangering health, and wrecking the natural world. Time and again, our boy George has made the billionaires' choice: corporate profits over public health.

8. **Iraq.** The Middle East has been an irritation to us billionaires for decades. Finally we've gone in and taken control. WMD, human rights, whatever—there's no need to complicate the issue. As long as our profit margins are healthy, we'll make it through.

Yes, the price in American lives is real. But 800-plus American and 10,000-plus Iraqi dead are a small price to pay for years of prosperity. These dead soldiers are noble patriots, dying for our way of life. ∎

JOHN KASCHT

CHAPTER II

The Business

We don't pay taxes.
Only the little people pay taxes.

—LEONA HELMSLEY

Less than Zero

*Moving toward a
negative corporate tax rate*

 ORPORATIONS ARE PEOPLE TOO, and it's an abomination to tax them twice. As long as we're still paying tax on our dividends, why should our companies pay tax on their profits too?

If your firm isn't doing what Texaco, PepsiCo, Pfizer, Enron, General Motors, Northrop Grumman, and more than 50 other multinationals are doing, you're paying for services that our American workers should be paying. Although these corporate citizens earn hundreds of millions (if not billions) of dollars in profits, they pay zero tax. Many fare far better than that, actually receiving *refunds* from the government, though the official corporate tax rate is 35 percent.

For example, in recent years:

• Over a three-year period, Texaco reported $3.4 billion in profits but qualified for tax rebates totaling $304 million.

The oil industry as a whole enjoyed a tax rate of only 5.7 percent—isn't that what they call "chump change"? And they aren't the only ones

Organizations We Love

CHAMBERS OF COMMERCE: Like volunteer branch offices promulgating our PR spin. Priceless.

FOX NEWS: Our own 24-hour shopping channel, with the world as our mom-and-pop shop. This network pumps our agenda nonstop every minute of the day—you can't beat it! Thank you, brother Murdoch! (Warning: priceless propaganda, but not a good channel to watch for actual "information" to plan your day by. Even the weather reports tilt to the right.)

continued

to have figured out how to make the Internal Revenue Service work for them:

- Texas-based El Paso Energy made $384 million but got back $3 million from the government.

- Chevron, which christened one of its tankers the *Condoleezza Rice*, earned $708 million in US profits, yet received a tax rebate of $187 million.

- Pfizer, purveyors of our beloved little blue pill, pocketed almost $200 million in tax rebates to add to a one-year profit of $1.2 billion.

- PepsiCo earned almost $1.6 billion and was refunded $302 million.

- After MCI WorldCom claimed a profit of $2.7 billion, the IRS slipped it a refund check for $112.6 million.

Hey, It's Not Our Pie!

Corporations are paying an ever-shrinking portion of the federal budget.

32%	21%	15%
1950s	1960s	1970s
10%	12%	7.4%
1980s	1990s	2000

- Colgate-Palmolive reaped $349 million in profits and almost $20 million in tax refunds.

- General Electric celebrated $6.9 billion in tax breaks over a three-year period.

HOW TO DO IT

- The law allows corporations to keep two sets of books: one for Wall Street, the other for the IRS—and lucky for us, they can have wildly diverging numbers.

- Shelter your profits by sending money abroad in "lease-in, lease-out" transactions. Offer to lease, say, sewer pipes in Bremen, Germany, at a cost of $20 million over ten years, and claim a business expense of half a billion dollars. Wachovia, a financial-services company, is king of the lease-in, lease-out deal, reporting $4 billion in profits in 2002, yet qualifying for $160 million in tax rebates.

- Learn all about "mark to market" accounting. Similar in some respects to lease-in, lease-out transactions, these contracts are designed to yield profits, if at all, only over a number of years. Then take it a step further by treating these hypothetical future gains as current profit, which you can use to justify astronomical stock prices and executive compensation.

"WISE USE" ENVIRONMENTALISTS: Fabulous folks. Main accomplishment: reclaiming the word *wise* for the cause of short-term profit maximalization in the wild. Thank Gaia there is no Lorax and the trees can't speak for themselves!

HERITAGE FOUNDATION: It's in our pockets, and it's helping to make those pockets deeper every day. The HF has funded every billionaire-positive "research project" you can think of. Global warming, taxation, whatever—the results always go our way.

CATO INSTITUTE: Hooray for (corporate) anarchy! These folks have put a

continued

- Hire an accounting firm to handle both your taxes and non-audit consulting work. That way it will likely look the other way (or, even better, actively aid you) in taking advantage of lax regulations. So much the better for you, with peace of mind, to freely defraud customers and investors. Enron retained Arthur Andersen, paying $25 million for auditing and $27 million for consulting. They got caught, but you don't have to.

- Outsource jobs to poor countries like India, Mexico, or China, where wages and tax rates are a fraction of what they are here, and there are no annoying labor unions to protect workers, no Social Security or Medicare payments, no child-labor laws. Best of all, the US government will offer you a tax incentive—as long as you keep the money abroad. Pfizer, for example, claimed $9 billion in "unrepatriated earnings" in 2002, which helped it shave its tax bill significantly. According to the Congressional Research Service, American corporations keep about $700 billion abroad in foreign unrepatriated earnings, which are not subject to the US tax code.

REVERSING THE SCOURGE OF DOUBLE TAXATION

Now, dear reader, it wasn't always thus. In a dark time not long ago, corporate income taxes made up 32 percent of federal tax receipts. That was 1952. Things have been looking up (and rates have been going down) ever since. By the '60s, 21 percent of federal revenues came from corporations; in the 1970s the figure dropped to 15 percent; and in 1983, with our supply-side savior, Ronald Wilson Reagan, at the helm, 10 percent.

Alas, under Bill Clinton the corporate tax share rose to more than 12 percent. But now, under the aegis of our fearless leader, George W. Bush, corporations are picking up just 7.4 percent of the nation's total tax bill. The amount of corporate tax revenue forgone in 2003 due to tax cuts enacted by George was about $60 billion, almost enough to pay for a year of war in Afghanistan, Iraq, and North Korea.

But wait! It gets better. Payroll taxes—which are levied on income from work, but not on interest, dividends, rent, capital gains, or any other form of our beloved investment income—made up 10 percent of all federal tax receipts in 1952, but today represent 40 percent. In essence, our investments in the Republican Party leadership have shifted the tax burden from corporations to the middle class, while at the same time cutting programs for the poor.

If we keep up our wise political investments, there is no reason to believe these trends won't continue. Corporations can look forward to paying a 0 percent share of the budget by the year 2008, and start enjoying a net *inflow* of Treasury Department cash thereafter. That's the kind of tax bracket we can live with!

— **Chase D. Gold / Adam Penenberg**

glimmer of intellectual respectability on our agenda. They are really helping us to make government small enough to strangle in the bathtub, as one of our friends so poetically put it.

INTERNATIONAL MONETARY FUND: The crowd here knows that austerity (like taxpaying) is for little people. They're keeping it real for us all over the world.

WORLD TRADE ORGANIZATION: Democracy can really interfere with the market—labor laws, environmental regulations. We've worked out a great "end run" strategy with the WTO, overruling all those pesky "laws" by fiat.

The Seven Habits of Highly Avaricious CEOs

1. **Make the pie higher!** When using fuzzy logic, call it "personal vision" and you can't be contradicted.

2. **Begin with the bottom line in mind.** Envision your life without money, shudder, and get to work.

3. **Put shiny things first.** Diamonds, gold, silver, the polish on a Rolls, the shine on a fine fur, life begins here.

4. **Think win/win, then think WIN WIN WIN WIN WIN!** Be assured that the other sucker's unprecedented losses guarantee your market domination.

5. **Seek first to understand, then to undermine.** Even when you're not in a zero-sum game, the top is always better.

6. **Push the envelope and grow your paradigm synergy.** To motivate and lead, coin arbitrary slogans and disseminate them authoritatively.

7. **Sharpen the dagger.** If you want a friend in this world, buy a puppy.

— Ike Horner de Marquette / Matthew Roth

Billionaires' Code of Conduct

E ARE LUCKY TO BE LIVING IN AN AGE OF unprecedented goodwill toward the wealthy and privileged. Yet still we see such language as "integrity," "ethics," and "principled behavior" in corporate codes of conduct. (Heck, they might even be in your own corporation's code!)

The Billionaires' Code of Conduct won't bore you with such vague and ephemeral terms. We shall cut to the chase: the wealthy are powerful, but small in number. Though we can afford to buy just about anything, we cannot afford to lose our finest citizens to silly business oversights that could have been avoided or, better yet, concealed. Getting caught simply has too many undesirable consequences:

• Time away from our business concerns, parties, and "significant others"

• Connubial visits from spouses

• Astronomical nannies' fees (doubly devastating when both caretakers face indictment)

• Gross devaluation of company stock

The Billionaires' Code of Conduct is not here to make you a better person. Rather, it demonstrates how, with a little knowledge and a tanker-full of creativity, we can stay within the confines of the laws we haven't bought yet.

Read. Absorb. Drink champagne.

— Mimi Mee / Hilary Hull

Greed is all right, by the way ... I think greed is healthy.
You can be greedy and still feel good about yourself.

— IVAN BOESKY

Insider Trading

*Making profits
and keeping them, too*

OBODY REALLY WANTS TO BREAK the law. Laws exist to protect our interests, for the most part. However, the degree to which the law is friend or foe largely depends on who's in the big chair in the Oval Office. Need we say more?

KEEPING SECRETS

Having to keep secrets is a terrible burden. Most of our secrets are those we are obliged to keep from our children, spouses, brothers and sisters, and yes, even Skull and Bones brethren—for their own good.

But if you hold a directorial position in your firm, you have a fiduciary duty *not* to give outsiders any information that might lead them to make very lucrative trades.

Insider-trading rules apply even if you've never set foot in your office since the day you inherited it and haven't the foggiest notion what your company does. But as we all know, fellow billionaires, behind every cloud lies a platinum lining, and the shimmering prize in this case comes from the most unlikely of sources: the SEC.

What's In Your Pockets?

Ticket stub from Rudy's skybox

Congressmen, lobbyists

Spare key to Ellen & Ron's Monaco pied-à-terre

Girlfriend's thong

Wife's Zoloft

Green Tic Tacs

The president

What's Not In Your Pockets?

Cash

Credit cards

Keys to the Volvo

Conscience

Our SEC has recently created a safe harbor that allows individuals to make trades while *in possession* of material and nonpublic information as long as they have a written, formal trading plan established before the trades are made.

THE SAFE HARBOR

You may develop a trading plan to sell stock when it reaches a certain price or at specified dates (for example, when payments of your children's college tuition are due). But best of all, you may terminate the trading plan at any time. I repeat, *at any time*. Who could blame you, then, for dumping your plan when a positive turn of events at your company just happens to coincide with the decision of all ten of your foster children to defer college for an indefinite period of time? Do you follow me?

(This preemptive plan may seem like a grand nuisance, but a dear friend of ours who was unable to produce said formal trading plan will soon be showing fellow inmates how to make hospital corners festive for the holidays.)

CONCLUSION

Insider-trading regulations are a hotbed of flimsy accusations and ludicrous convictions. Government enforcers need them because their lives are meaningless, and they would otherwise never see the insides of our homes. So stay ahead of the game—make a game plan.

— Mimi Mee / Hilary Hull

CODE OF CONDUCT, PART III

In Trust We Trust

*Keeping their laws out of
your inferences*

NTITRUST LAWS HAVE OFTEN been referred to as "unfair-competition laws." We could not agree more. It hardly seems fair for the government to thwart the healthy growth of conglomerates in favor of brash young upstarts.

But the injustice hardly stops there. In other areas of the law, "innocent until proven guilty" is the guiding principle.

Not so in antitrust cases. The mere *inference* of suspicious activities by you or your most trusted employees is enough to slap you with a federal offense.

To protect yourself from persecution, you must construct every corporate communication as though hostile government enforcement authorities are peering over your shoulder, threatening you with the prospect of bedside urinals and group therapy with the sort of people you've only seen portrayed on TV. It's either that, or invest in a top-notch paper shredder.

But controllable, written communication isn't

Billionaire Jokes

Why did the billionaire cross the road?

His holding company had a lien on the chicken.

What did one CEO with labor troubles say to the other CEO with labor troubles?

"Take my strife, please."

Why did the elephant get stuck in the bathtub?

No billionaire, radio.

Why are there no oil magnates who are bartenders?

They can't tell the difference between Tanqueray and "Tanker B."

– 73 –

your greatest concern. It's the inferences that will really take the bubbles out of your Cristal.

What, then, constitutes an inference? Juries enjoy limitless authority to misinterpret any of the following:

- A "knowing" wink or nod.

- Casual use of phrases such as "aligning operations," "stabilization," or "industry consensus."

- Private meetings in a hotel among a few old friends whose companies just happen to dominate the market they compete in.

- Coincidental raising or lowering of prices, refusals to purchase from a common supplier, or limitations on production by two competitors immediately after a trade meeting.

So does this mean you must refrain from any communication with competitors? Hardly! If that were the case, our country-club dinners would be silent. Consider these alternatives:

INSTEAD OF A WINK OR A NOD . . .

It seems only subtle gestures have been tagged as signs of an illicit agreement. As far as we know, no one's ever had to testify on account of:

- Involuntary twitches such as ear wiggling, or arching one eyebrow and then the second, the second again and then the first, and back again.

- Chronic shadow boxing.

- An impromptu performance of *Riverdance* on the floor of the stock exchange.

NO HIGH-PROFILE MEETING LOCALES . . .

Sports-arena hospitality suites and offshore vacation spots are the first places the Feds will come looking for you. However, they'll never expect to find you at:

- A woodworking class offered by your local community college.

- A lecture on sustainable agriculture.

- The waiting room at H&R Block.

ON MISLEADING LANGUAGE . . .

You may have been referring to the liner notes of your favorite Perry Como album when overheard uttering the phrase "strictly off the record" to a competitor, but these words sound quite different to a judge with a lively imagination. We suggest you code your conversations with topics so tiresome that even the most tenacious of eavesdroppers will nod off before finding out what you're really discussing. To wit:

- Top ten commentaries heard on *All Things Considered*

- Universal health care

More Billionaire Jokes

Two billionaires are walking down the street when one turns to the other: "Tell me the truth, were you happier when you were poor?" "I was happier when I was poor," the second billionaire replies. "But I was so poor I was miserable."

A billionaire, an arms dealer, and a stock-broker walk into a bar. The billionaire says, "I'll have a Manhattan." So the arms dealer says, "Oh yeah, well, I'll have a kamikaze." Not to be outdone, the stockbroker says, "I'll have what they're having."

— Jon Dellheim and Kurt Opprecht

- *Forward Drive: The Race to Build the Clean Car of the Future* by Jim Motavalli

If all else fails, try pig Latin. Why? Imagine how credible a witness would sound repeating that on the stand.

JUST SAY "WHAT?" ...

But what if it's someone else who initiates the suspicious communication? At this point in your company's code of conduct, you probably advise your employees to:

- Say NO,
- GO, and
- TELL your company's legal department

—worthwhile advice for those without a refined sense of business protocol. But that's not us. Let your associates say what they will. It's your duty to feign incomprehension. Any non sequitur will do:

- "I hate to be the one to tell you this, but you have some caviar stuck between your teeth."
- "Yes, but the letter Q falls on a triple letter score."
- "Look! Someone dropped a penny over by the Monet."
- "Eggplant? I love eggplant. Where's my seamstress?"

— Mimi Mee / Hilary Hull

Offshoring: The New Outsourcing

Labor arbitrage in five easy steps

SHIPPING BLUE-COLLAR JOBS OVERSEAS replaced indentured servitude as the mainstream personnel strategy in the 1970s, but as jobs grew more sophisticated in the '80s, it began to look as though profits would again be held hostage to labor costs. With the advent of the Internet and large numbers of educated poor, how-ever, business barons discovered the key to unbridled wealth: white-collar slavery (more elegantly termed "offshoring").

Sadly, only a handful of corporations are tapping the full potential that offshoring can bring to the bottom line. Moving jobs overseas can be problematic for employee morale and may attract unwanted intervention by politicians. At times it may seem more trouble than it's worth. Thus, in the interest of advancing the GDP, we offer:

THE BILLIONAIRES FOR BUSH FIVE-STEP PLAN FOR FUN AND PROFITABLE OFFSHORING
1. Start with "managed attrition." To minimize panic among employees you still need, begin early and stage layoffs in shifts that appear to

Sample Weekly Budget
DUES
Country club: $200
Yacht club: $300
Union League club: $2,500
PBA: $18

Alimony (both): $15,000

Child support (domestic): $30,000/ month each

Child support (international): $2,500/month each

UNDERLINGS

Personal assistant, caddie, valet, chef, driver: $1,500

Body-enhancement specialist: $2,000

"Nanny": $600

Mansion staff: $1,200

continued

be natural attrition. When you fill these vacancies abroad, you can claim that no jobs were lost.

2. Say "offshoring" instead of "outsourcing." It sounds more temporary, as though the jobs are being sent on a vacation (as in "I'm offshoring in the yacht this weekend").

3. Raise desperation and lower salaries. With the threat of layoffs hanging over their heads and the fear that their jobs will be sent overseas, your personnel will become refreshingly eager to accept pay cuts and longer hours. Heck, they'll likely be too scared to take paid vacations!

4. Offshore with a smile. The business press loves news of offshoring, so make sure coverage of your personnel strategy is handled by Wall Street media, not the local press. Be positive when you break the news. Employees may complain about having to train their foreign replacements, but you can cast it as an opportunity to make friends abroad. Reinforce the idea that better jobs will soon be created for them in booming industries such as nanotechnology, bioinformatics, and food service.

5. Reinvest your profits. Once the offshoring is complete, you might be tempted to relax with the knowledge that your overseas operation is raising your revenues at one third the cost. But to diminish criticism in the business press and keep the doors open to cheap labor, you must continually reinvest in media outlets. Also, remember your "elected" officials: they're the only people you can't offshore.

Don't miss the boat. Remember: if you're not offshoring, you could be the next to be offshored! — Owen Dwight Howse / D. M. Rider

Remember Your Norvir

Make a killing in health care the Abbott Laboratories way

ARE YOU TIRED OF THE RIGORS of free-market capitalism? Of spending your own money on product development? Of underperforming investments and customers who are free to take their business elsewhere?

Follow *The Norvir Plan* for financial success in the pharmaceutical industry, and you and your relatives may never have to rely on sound business practices again! Pills + Patents = Profits. Remember your Norvir.

THE NORVIR PLAN

Step 1: Enter a product market where the alternative to treatment is slow, painful death. It's way easier to negotiate prices with customers who are going to die a slow, painful death if they don't take your medicine. Time is an important element in every negotiation, and in this case, time is on your side.

Step 2: Have the government pay to develop the product. Why should pharmaceutical companies be burdened with financing research

Chateau staff: $900

Private-island staff: $1,500

Third-World-country staff: $10

OFF BOOKS
Mistress's clothing allowance: $4,000 in peak social season, $2,000 out of season

Mistress's apartment: New York, $1,000 Paris, $1,100

Mistress's Pilates instructor: $1,100

Local congressman: $1,200

Local senator: $12,000

Hush money: $10,500

Kickbacks: $1,600

OTHER NEEDS
Massages, dancers, "company," happy endings:

continued

"Billions, DAMMIT! Not millions."

when the National Institutes of Health can be persuaded to pick up the tab? Taxpayers love the NIH, and the NIH loves drugs, which is why the NIH sponsors National Cooperative Drug Discovery Groups to encourage private development of medical treatments, and why, between 1988 and 1993, Abbott Laboratories received a multi-year NCDDG grant to work on an AIDS treatment involving HIV protease enzymes.

Step 3: Get over it. Sharing is for losers. Once a medicine is developed at taxpayers' expense, claim proprietary rights to all research-related patents.

Public funding of a private business venture shouldn't obligate you to share the resulting intellectual property with the public, or with the public-health professionals who act in its interest. Your obligation is to the health of your bottom line. Abbott Labs used its federal grant money to develop ritonavir, marketed as Norvir. Norvir is a financial blockbuster for the company, but Abbott fought to keep the intellectual property all to itself.

Karl Marx said that all property is theft. We have proved him wrong again. All theft is property, especially in the pharmaceutical industry.

Step 4: Obey the law of supply and demand. Once you have supplied thousands with a drug they depend on for their survival, demand a heart-stopping price increase just as gross sales go over $1 billion.

After topping the $1 billion mark with Norvir, Abbott raised its wholesale price by 400 percent in late 2003, from $54 to $265 for a month's supply.

Step 5: Put your purchasing power to work. Today's billionaire CEOs must look for the highest returns from health-care-related ventures. We cannot cease our lobbying for business-friendly reform. Free-market-based health-care legislation, like corporate subsidies and non-negotiation clauses that benefit private over public interests, is a start—only a start. After all, the story of Norvir is just one example of how high profits save lives.

— Skip S. Tate-Tax / Patrick Nash

Las Vegas, $15,000
Everywhere else, $1,500

Table retainer at Daniel: $150

Food and litter for kids' elephant: $524

Helicopter (personal, not the corporate one): $3,700

Catamaran maintenance and crew: $3,500

Cheetos: $56

Antibacterial soaps/disinfectants: $1,400

Chump change: $1,400

Mani-pedi, Botox, hair-plug updates: $800

Meds: $1,289

Library fines: $75

A Billionaire's Guide to the Universe

The Carlyle Nebula

I N THE UNIVERSE OF COSMIC CAPITALISM, AT THE FAR reaches of regulation and public understanding, dark matter and the hidden connections between powerful forces conspire to make heavenly profits. For years, far from our gaze, one radiant cloud has lit up fortunes from Washington to London, Riyadh to Rome—the Carlyle Nebula.

We still don't know exactly what this mass of billions and billions of dollars is, what forces it controls, or whether one day it might destroy us. But we do know this: it thrives on chaos and war, building big guns to attack infinite enemies. It uses the gravitational pull of its big stars—ex-presidents, prime ministers, secretaries of defense and state—to extract luminous paydays from public tills. It does strange things with human matter, as government officials vanish and eerily rematerialize as Carlyle execs. It sucks the light of public scrutiny into the black hole of denial and secrecy. Mysteriously, it expands by contracting: lots of contracts, all over the world, between governments, investors, and the companies it owns or represents.

Some of the Stars

Frank Carlucci, former chairman
Former secretary of defense and deputy director of CIA. Was Rummy's roommate and wrestling-team pal at Princeton. Wrote letters to his Princeton buddy and to Colin Powell lobbying for certain (Carlyle-friendly?) changes in defense planning.

George Bush Sr., senior adviser
Former prez; father of our favorite idiot savant; Carlyle jet-setter with major ties to royal families.

James Baker, senior counselor
Former secretary of state and treasury. Defense lawyer for Saudis who were sued by families of 9/11 victims for alleged terrorist ties.

John Major, chairman of Carlyle Europe
Former prime minister of Britain. Recently Carlyle bought—and hence privatized—the UK's Ministry of Defense Research Agency. It also bought from Fiat a company that does high-tech work for Italy's Defense Department.

David Rubenstein, cofounder
Once a hardworking progressive policy wonk serving under President Carter, Rubenstein is now a fabulously wealthy man with vacation homes throughout America. He safaris with Barbara Bush and voted GOP in 2000.

Telescopes, in the hands of intrepid journalists and public-interest groups, are just starting to make out the contours of this nebulous nebula.

Largely through United Defense Industries, the Carlyle Group is the eleventh-largest US defense contractor.

Never until George Bush Sr. came along was a former president financially involved in the defense industry. As a Carlyle bigwig, Pops stands to gain financially from the hawkishness of his son. (Not hard to peddle influence on one's kid, wethinks.) Senior has advised Junior on policy in the Middle East and the Koreas. Carlyle has extensive investments in the Middle East and South Korea.

Carlyle is mainly a private equity firm that buys and sells private companies and divisions of large public companies.

The bin Laden family had investments in a Carlyle fund for six years. After 9/11 they withdrew their money, as some noted that they might profit from the actions of their renegade relative Osama (with whom they reportedly cut ties years ago).

These big stars shoot around the world, meeting with kings, princes, ministers, and investors. When they speak, people listen—and open their wallets to invest. They get handsomely paid for their words: former president Bush earns as much as $100,000 per engagement.

— Merchant F. Arms / Jeremy Varon

Fifteen men on the dead man's chest.
Yo-ho-ho, and a bottle of rum! Drink and the devil had
done for the rest. Yo-ho-ho, and a bottle of rum!

— ROBERT LOUIS STEVENSON
TREASURE ISLAND

What Money?

Offshoring your company's big bucks

AX TIME USED TO BE A ROYAL NUISANCE for billionaires. There are so many rules and regulations in the tax code, it's no wonder former Treasury Secretary Paul O'Neill once described it as "9,500 pages of gibberish." Why, it was almost easier to pay some taxes than to avoid them! Fortunately, all that has changed.

Kate Barton of the accounting firm Ernst & Young presents a visionary tax strategy that really makes sense from the billionaire's point of view. It's called "corporate inversion": sort of a fiscal shell game for CEOs to play for the IRS.

With corporate inversion, we can take full advantage of all America has to offer, including access to its markets, its well-educated workforce, and its infrastructure. The American military protects our foreign interests, and American law-enforcement agencies protect our wealth and property at home. They even enforce the patents that we use to prevent competition and keep prices high. And it's all free, because it's financed through payroll taxes collected from our middle-class and working-class employees!

Over the next ten years the richest 1 percent of Americans will each get a $500,000 care package from our president, for a total of $1.1 trillion! And that's just to individuals; it doesn't include what he's giving to our corporations. The icing on the cake: we can now use the debt and deficit to justify slashing spending on Social Security, health care, and all those other terrible New Deal programs that put people before corporations.

⚓

Follow Kate's advice and watch the IRS try to get you.

1. Subsidiarize. Have your corporation create an offshore subsidiary. You may choose from any number of tropical resort islands, but one of our favorite setups is a Bermuda-based subsidiary with legal residence in Barbados. There's no need to worry about office space or production costs, let alone actually relocating. The subsidiary need be nothing more than a mailbox and a few documents in a file cabinet.

2. Move the moolah. Once your corporation has established its subsidiary, transfer ownership of the real company to the imaginary, offshore company. It's like adopting a child in a Third World country and then having that child declare you as a dependent on his income tax. That's the inversion.

3. Extraction. At this point, the imaginary company (the one that you own and is not subject to US taxes) can extract enormous fees from the real company (the one that you own and is subject to US taxes). Be creative. In addition to rent and leases, the offshore company can charge for licensing intellectual property, such as the product name or company logo.

Through such creative invoicing, the real company's profits are siphoned off in fees paid to the imaginary company. The fees appear as expenses in the US, while they pile up as profits in your bank account in Bermuda!

What about taxes in Bermuda, you say? Well, with this setup, the effective corporate tax rate for the offshore entity is about 1 percent. Compare that with the US rate of 35 percent, and it's easy to see why so many corporations are choosing to move their ownership offshore.

WHERE TO DO IT

Of the many wealth-friendly nations in the world, there is perhaps none so famous as the Cayman Islands. It's a real tribute to the vision of the American CEO that this minuscule nation, with virtually no resources or indigenous commerce, has grown to rival such historically great banking centers as Zurich, New York, Hong Kong, and London. In 1996 there were approximately 27,000 businesses registered there. That's about one for each resident. Not bad for an island whose neighbors include Cuba and Haiti.

DOWNSIDES?

Occasionally our friends in the media cast these tax havens in a negative light, claiming it's unfair to shelter profits in the protections of the US tax code while diverting money from the US Treasury. Even some CEOs have felt the weight of this media smear campaign. But fear not: as long as the Bushes are in power, you'll be in good company. While Dick Cheney was its CEO, Halliburton created not one but 20 subsidiaries in the Cayman Islands. Even George, as a director of Harken Energy in 1989, was involved in the creation of an offshore subsidiary that could have sheltered profits if Harken had ever earned any. — Skip S. Tate-Tax / Patrick Nash

Under Bush's tenure, the Environmental Protection Agency has dropped 62 environmental standards enacted by previous administrations to protect the public health. As a result of the White House's refusal to enforce environmental-protection laws against its wealthy campaign contributors (that's you and me!), the EPA's two most senior enforcement officials resigned after decades of work.

Waste Not, Profit Not

Management plan

NOTE: *Legislation is pending. This is only a rough blueprint.*

SECTION I: LAND/WATER

Nothing is actually "garbage" until it leaves the factory loading dock. After that, it is society's problem, and our opportunity. Over the past decade, liability for products destined for Consumer Retail Market Specimens (CRMS, or "crumbs") has been effectively eliminated, thus permitting industrial waste to be conveyed to the consumer in the form of bulky, eye-catching, non-recyclable packaging. The crumb opens his shiny new toothbrush package, beer can, or egg carton and *voilà*, he acquires responsibility for disposing of plastic, cadmium, mercury, bleached paper pulp, etc.

When their quarter-acre parcels of the American dream butt up against such waste repositories as may be required, and crumbs initiate actions to protect their health or safety, grants shall be duly offered to their leaders to quell controversy.

SECTION II: AIR

For all intents and purposes, relief of liability for damage to air is not an area that requires much additional work. Present and past legislation permits those of us who do not pollute enough to sell "pollution credits" to firms that poison more than their fair share of crumbs. (Worry not, my friends, for on a clear day the haze of midtown Manhattan never reaches Martha's Vineyard.) Moreover, there isn't a crumb to speak of who possesses the air-sampling facilities needed to challenge the findings of our Environmental Protection racket (Agency). This makes our word final and renders court challenges over the existence or effect of supposed "toxins" moot.

SECTION III: ENERGY BYPRODUCTS, CONTAMINANTS

God bless the army of Willy Lomans who blanketed this country with power lines and subsidized electricity decades ago. Tobacco-like dependence on our valuable wattage sets a crumb convulsing when his TV/toasteroven/tuna-can opener goes on the blink. Keeping their TV dinners hot, whether through nuclear, coal, or diesel-fired turbines, keeps us in ermine and Montecristos. Making sure it all stays that way, however, is not yet a given.

During its first term, the Bush II administration has mitigated liability from the production of countless hazardous byproducts of energy generation. Yet we need to ensure that liability for our future ventures is appropriately conveyed to the crumbs, that is, civil society. We can earn our due while society is merrily pacified into perpetuity if we deliver the remaining industrial liabilities to the following repositories:

- **Contaminated fuel oil:** Fuel tanks of suburban homes

- **Coal residue and ash:** Mixed with concrete, deposited in rural roadbeds and offshore underwater reefs

- **Nuclear waste:** Nevada sand pits

- **Other heavy metals:** Low-tar cigarettes

— Matt Reiss

Global Domestication

Blueprint for the species

ITH PRESERVATION OF OUR persons and property an increasingly crucial part of our daily routine, the Corporate/Government Partnership (i.e., White House) has issued the second installment of its two-phase plan for ensuring that property accumulation remains safe from weather damage, expropriation by popular majority, or natural selection.

Phase one, 2000-2004: By the end of this phase, unrestrained hydrocarbon emissions will have successfully converted the temperate North American climate into income-enhancing desert conditions (a utilities-friendly, two-part heating/AC cycle), while managed deforestation will have successfully curbed the spread of indigenous plant life.

Phase two, 2004-2008: It is estimated that the Partnership will require four additional years to lift remaining regulatory restrictions to the complete elimination of free-range wildlife (see management plan below).

Profit-Maximized Wildlife-Management Plan

KINGDOM, VEGETABLE; SPECIES, INDIGENOUS FLORA

All plant chromosome structures shall be licensed to the highest bidder. (The winning bid may be eligible for grants and subsidies from the Department of Agriculture.) Following a three-month period of public notification, the cultivation of, ingestion of, or oxygenation from these species will be restricted to that permitted by the licensee.

KINGDOM, ANIMAL; PHYLUM, MAMMAL

In the wild, travels in packs and has a sophisticated pecking order. As a result, this phylum can be easily manipulated to follow a dominant member. The master should speak softly to it, pet it, and overfeed it until a bond between the keeper and the creature is attained. It must then be broken of spirit, isolated from the herd, and weaned of its need for natural environment. Successful domestication of this phylum has been achieved when it responds obediently to the sound of its master's voice.

KINGDOM, DOMESTIC ANIMAL; SPECIES, HOMO MIDDLE AMERICUS

In the wild, travels in packs and has a sophisticated pecking order. As a result, this species can be easily manipulated to follow a dominant member or prerecorded message. The master should speak softly to it, pet it, and overfeed it until a bond between the keeper and the creature is attained. It must then be broken of spirit, isolated from the herd, and weaned of its need for natural environment. Successful domestication of this species has been achieved when it responds obediently to network broadcasts.   — Matt Reiss

*It is not the employer who pays the wages.
Employers only handle the money. It is the customer
who pays the wages.*

— HENRY FORD

Scorched-Earth Retailing

The Wal-Mart assault model

I F CONSUMER CULTURE IS THE fuel that America's economy runs on, then workers' rights and benefits are the sand in the crankcase. Health insurance, higher wages, OSHA, and other regrettable trends of the last century have really begun to dig into retailers' bottom lines. Fortunately, Wal-Mart's brazen business model is turning back the clock on the more damaging workers' rights trends and, thankfully, ridding our heartland of the scourge of mom-and-pop stores.

Here's how to follow that plan and get your selling machine running clean:

1. Fight the good fight for lower wages and benefits. Companies like General Motors fueled the growth of the world's most affluent middle class by paying higher-than-average wages and offering generous health-care packages to their workers. These corrosive "wage patterns" forced other companies to raise their compensation levels, giving birth to the old "rising tides raise all ships" adage that we've been preaching for years. In a time of rising costs for health care,

Synergy In Action
Wal-Mart's Deft One-Two Punch

A t Wal-Mart, every register is recorded at all times, its performance stored down there at company headquarters in Arkansas. These records are analyzed and audited frequently to zero in on any employee showing slow performance. One store manager bragged that he could look up "last year, July 12, how much in sales the store did and how much was rung up by Sally Jo, the cashier, within a particular hour." With such oversight, under-performing employees are

continued

tuition, gas, and real estate, Wal-Mart's workers average less than $18,000 a year! Wal-Mart extends the olive branch of health insurance to its staff, but here's the brilliant catch: it charges so much for coverage that one third of its workers choose not to have it!

2. Choke out the competition. Once a Wal-Mart moves in, smaller, less aggressive independent retailers that can't compete with its global buying power and low prices have no recourse but to close up shop. Regional hegemony gives Wal-Mart immense power over its employees. Couple this monopoly with Step 3 and you have one hell of an efficient (cheap) workforce.

3. Micromanage. From its headquarters in Bentonville, Arkansas, Wal-Mart has fused electronic surveillance with

micromanagement in effective ways. Integrating all aspects of its operation back to Bentonville, corporate software tracks every register to monitor employee performance, counts every piece of inventory, and even controls the indoor temperature in each one of its 3,500 US stores. Ready access to these numbers allows Wal-Mart to bully suppliers for lower prices, weed out slacker employees, and predict buying trends before they even happen.

4. Stuff! If things are so bad for the middle class, you ask, why don't they complain? It's simple: consumers prefer low prices at the marketplace to fairness in the workplace. *Stuff*, of all things. It was that easy all along. Marx was wrong: it is stuff, and not just stuff, but the deluge of *new stuff*, that is the opiate of the masses, the classes, and the American economic miracle.

Annual sales of $256 billion prove these tactics have worked better than Wal-Mart's wildest dreams. More chains are emulating the model every quarter. We know yours will soon, if it's still around.

— Monet Oliver d'Place / Marco Ceglie

warned to either speed up or hit the road and find another job—but Wal-Mart has forced out all the other jobs, so the employee has to put up with low wages, fixed high-cost health insurance, long hours, and anti-union policies (Wal-Mart is nearly 40 percent family-owned, bless its heart). Add to this President Bush's recent drive to cut those eligible for overtime pay, and we've got labor conditions even we would feel guilty exploiting. (No, we don't—huzzah!)

FACTOID
Wal-Mart is the largest employer in 21 of the 50 states.

It is said that the world is in a state of bankruptcy,
that the world owes the world more than the world can pay.

— RALPH WALDO EMERSON

Covering Your Assets

Bankruptcy for billionaires

IT'S A GIVEN THAT IF YOU'RE NOT racking up some sizable debt loads, you're not playing the game right. Sure, you get behind the eight ball once in a while. That's why we made the rules of the game to keep the creditors out of your corner pocket, side pocket, and vest pocket. You know the word: bankruptcy.

In any of the six domestic wealth havens, you can protect your "homestead"—a property of unlimited value—even as you declare Chapter 7 bankruptcy and send creditors packing.

If you're a bit shy of the stigma, just follow the example of a good number of our number who have done their part to render wealthy bankruptcy utterly shameless:

Abe Gosman, health-care and real-estate magnate, declared bankruptcy in Florida, citing debts of more than $233 million. Nonetheless, he was able to hold onto his 64,000-square-foot mansion in West Palm Beach on a street known as "Billionaire's Row."

Marvin Warner, who owned a failed Ohio

Profiles In Plastic

Cash 'n' carry— qu'est-ce que c'est?

emember back when our favorite credit cards magically turned gold, then platinum? Well, the pace of change is quickening. The "new" Amex Black Card will soon be as passé as Manolo Blahniks. Here's a preview of the next few rungs up the plastic ladder:

THE STRATO CARD

So exclusive it doesn't even exist. You can't apply for it. There's nothing to join. You either have it or you don't. Merely whisper the words. There's nothing to carry,

"Well, hello there...I'm liquid."

savings and loan, paid off only a fraction of his $300 million debt while keeping his multimillion-dollar horse ranch near Ocala, Florida.

Corporate raider Paul Bilzerian kept his $5 million Florida home while completely ditching $200 million in debt. (This guy's a pro—he's filed for bankruptcy twice!)

Even Burt Reynolds got into the act. He kept his $2.5

million home while paying his creditors 20 cents on the dollar.

Yes, in the past few years anti-wealth legislators have tried to revise the federal bankruptcy laws more than once, and the Senate has specifically targeted these precious homestead exemptions. But we needn't worry; each effort has failed miserably. We have powerful allies, including our darling Dubya.

The states themselves aren't likely to repeal the protections anytime soon. Florida and Texas have made the exemption a constitutional right—can't get safer than that. (Thank heaven for "conservative" approaches to constitutional amendments.)

If you're holding back on purchases for fear of running up a deficit that rivals the Fed's, take solace in the books, websites, and law firms all dedicated to helping us make the most of bankruptcy. Indeed, people move to these places just to take advantage of these laws.

Remember, there's no more effective (or enjoyable) insurance policy against a delinquent heir or desperate plaintiffs trying to collect their billion-dollar judgment than a grandiose estate in West Palm Beach.

— Anastasia Romanov / Abigail Caplovitz

nothing to sign. You won't leave home without it because you can't.

THE STL CARD

The "Sky's The Limit" with this little beauty, but the minimum purchase is a cool million. Not for every day, but perfect for small islands, movie studios, corporate takeovers, and "exploratory" drilling in Arctic wilderness.

THE EMPEROR'S CARD

Invisible to those not worthy; only members of our class and our "people" will ever know you have this fine instrument. If you can't see it, you don't deserve to see it.

— M.P. Dunleavey

Where Charity Begins and Ends

Strategic donation

THANKFULLY, THE BUSH II ADMINISTRATION has done exactly what we've paid it to do: decrease our personal and corporate taxes. Although we are grateful, we should bear in mind that our taxes have not yet been eliminated completely. So what is a billionaire to do come tax day?

Giving to charity not only provides opportunities for tax deductions; it also offers more intangible gratification. A hefty donation provides the satisfaction of knowing you are helping your fellow man. In other words, being the "good guy."

But not every donation will be viewed as appropriate or laudable. There are many who view public gifts as treason to our class. So how is a billionaire to navigate the quagmire of charitable organizations clamoring for a handout? One should keep a few general concepts in mind, based on the following examples:

GREEN PIECE
Say your country club is having its annual Bridge Club Beautification Day, and your third

wife decides to donate $25,000. The club receives your generous patronage, everything looks lovely, and you've earned admiration from fellow members. This is a good choice. However, since clubs are generally not considered charities (although you *are* performing a charitable act), the gift would not provide any benefits at tax time.

GREENER PIECE

Let's say you completed the above but, in addition, decided that your efforts would be much more substantial if the financial rewards were going to a good cause. In that case, *leverage* the gift for the beautification by persuading the club to allow you to host a benefit golf tournament. The ample greens fees would, of course, be distributed in part to the club, but, by donating a larger portion, you would reap the tax benefits. A good deed turns into a good margin. But there are still better ways to perfect this concept.

HEALTH RELIEF

You're the chairman of the board at a large pharmaceutical company. Create an endowment for victims of an illness that your company could profit from, specifically for medical research. Use your golf tournament to raise money for that charity, thereby funding your own charity—which is actually doing research for your company—to develop products sold through Medicare at a 300 percent profit. *Voilà!* Not only does it appear that you are generous, but you have found a way to pay for research, get a tax break, and increase your standing in the eyes of your peers as a generous individual and/or corporation! Welcome to the world of the savvy charitable billionaire!   — D. Prescott Windavit / Scott Faucheux

One of the great attractions of patriotism is it fulfills our worst wishes. In the person of our nation we are able, vicariously, to bully and cheat. Bully and cheat, what's more, with a feeling that we are profoundly virtuous.

— ALDOUS HUXLEY

The Ethicist

*Expert advice for your
most delicate fiduciary dilemmas*

Dear Randy,

Earlier this year, during an exclusive event off the coast of Hilton Head, a band of masked bandits motored up in a speedboat and boarded our yacht.

The thieves demanded we hand over all of our cash and other valuables. Just then I remembered that I owed my personal assistant a year of back pay. So I pulled out my wallet and handed him ten crisp $100 bills on the spot. The bandits took it immediately, of course, but now I'm wondering: how should I report his pay to the IRS?

Donald, The
New York, NY

Dear Donald,

Well, first of all, thinking of your trusty manservant in a crisis like that proves you've got a big heart as well as a large wallet.

Good show!

As for the IRS, worry not. For payments of up to $1,000, it's up to the laborer to report his wages.

ur critics complain that as we consolidate media ownership into fewer and fewer hands, it threatens "diversity." Well, the spin cycle isn't over, folks. Consolidation is a *means* of diversification.

MORE CHANNELS = MORE CHOICES!

The media conglomerate is the cultural clearinghouse for the industry, preventing the redundancies inherent in locally owned radio, television, and print. Consolidation ensures one each of all relevant tastes and styles, whatever the genre: country or western, sitcom or game show, right-wing or middle-of-the-road.

continued

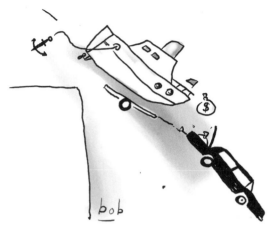

bob

"AHHHHHHHHHH!!!!!
I'M TAKING IT ALL WITH MEEEEEE!!!

Dear Randy,

I am the CEO of an automobile company. These days it's far more profitable to move all our factories overseas than to keep them running in the United States. In China, for example, orphans are willing to work for slave wages, and the neo-Stalinist government keeps them in line. However, this opportunity has created an ethical problem: do we close our American factories and sell the assets immediately? Or should we create a front company to purchase our former factory assets in the United States at wildly inflated prices, allowing me to cash in on stock-market gains before the truth is discovered?

Busta U. Nyun
Flint, MI

Dear Busta,

Either way, you must act quickly. If you don't close your US-based factories immediately, investors will lose confidence in your decisiveness. Stock prices in your real company will plummet. The front company is a delicious idea, but it's better to save it for a business that is actually failing, such as "allegedly" occurred with Harken Energy in the late '8os.

Dear Randy,

I used to head an oil and gas firm in Texas, but now I'm the vice president of a major super-power. I still receive a deferred salary from my former company and continue to hold 433,333 shares in stock options. This compensation is on top of my $20 million retirement package.

Admittedly, it's a paltry sum, but now I am in a position to help this company receive billions in government contracts. This creates the following ethical dilemma: do I need to share any of my deferred salary or stock options with the president?

Dick
Undisclosed Location

Dear Dick,

Your influence put you in the position of power you're now enjoying. Now is not the time to start sharing and giving. Just think about it this way: you'd be setting a dangerous precedent for the president!

— **Drillmore Wells / David Hyde**

DIVERSITY OF OPINION
A properly filtered range of opinion is merely one of the services media con-glomeration brings to the table. Having too many ideas con-fuses the audience and tends to draw consumer focus away from our corporate sponsors' products.

MERCANTILE DIVERSITY
Every demographic has its own shopping and consuming habits. Never have there been more products pitched. Further consolidation will allow further diversification: one shopping network devoted to Elvis memorabilia, another that caters to the Dogs Playing Poker crowd, etc.

— Felonious T. Axe / Clifford Tasner

Making a Living
Making a Killing

Avuncular advice

My Dear Harold,

On the occasion of your graduation, along with my enclosed check I offer advice on where your holdings might find a happy home: blast off into missile defense, Harold. That's the wave of the future.

Remember freshman economics? Great. Now forget it. Demand is fleeting. Supply is the law. You eliminate the middleman when the nukes are aimed at the consumer. With MD, the returns are all "cost plus," and the "plus" is where you and I come in.

It was touch-and-go back in the '80s, with Gorbachev damning our prospects. If reformers like him had their way, Uncle Sam might have no enemies at all, Harold. And you know that's not good for business. But thanks to our friend Dick Cheney, we remain in the game.

You remember Dick, don't you? He was the rather carnivorous gentleman at the family barbecue. If it weren't for him, there would be no investment-grade opportunities in defense contracting. There'd be little interest in infrared optics, armored satellites, or exo-atmospheric kill vehicles. Certainly no R&D pass/fail guarantees. Damn sure, no more no-bid contracts. Hell, the defense budget wouldn't be a tenth of what it is now without Dick.

Back during the Cold War, with all the world focused on the Russkies, Mr. Cheney kept his head and cultivated other opportunities for war profits. You're too young to remember when Pyongyang cooled the fuel rods in 1989, and chipped off enough boom-boom to make warheads. But we at the club toasted our Dick.

When the veep lifted safeguards and pushed Russia and China into multilateral talks last year, it managed to buy Little Kim enough time to carve off sufficient boom-boom for another half-dozen mushroom clouds. (Remind me to send a fruit basket to the National Press Club for keeping the cat in the bag, will you?) Like the longhairs used to say, "You have to have an enemy to justify expenditures on weapons." Well, Dick is making sure that we'll have enemies galore for years to come.

Missile-defense money is guaranteed for a good 30 years, whether or not we still have the Bush brothers and Congress on retainer. So talk to me about leasing an office in Arlington and hire a couple of buzz-cuts to fill out forms. Ex-defense chiefs are pricey, but any general with a pension should do—gray, khaki, or Navy blue. (Remember, three stars equals "investment grade.") Tell them to pick up their conflict-of-interest waivers at the office by the commissary.

Harry, you're a bright lad. A chip off the family tree. I'm sure I don't need to say more. Enjoy your graduation parties, and don't bother to top off the tanks on the jet. This trip's on me!

See you at the club.

Your Loving Uncle

— Matt Reiss

ERIC PALMA

CHAPTER III

The Life

Does it really matter what these affectionate people do, so long as they don't do it in the street and frighten the horses?

— MRS. PATRICK CAMPBELL

Billionaires in Bed

Grubstakes for Gold Diggers

S WE BILLIONAIRES ARE WELL aware, our inferiors like to speculate about how to get us into bed and what we like to do there. Rarely, however, do they guess accurately. (Chiefly because sex simply does not mean to billionaires what it does to commoners.)

While sex can be a pleasure, it is life's greatest pleasure only for those who don't own villas, media empires, or thoroughbreds. For most of us chosen few, the really big billions don't roll in until after 50, and by then we have, frankly, more erotic things to do—like penetrating new markets, watching our big billions make little billions, or, like Enron's Kenneth Lay, getting our company's figures massaged by our accountants. Frisky middle-class people may swing, but frisky billionaires swing elections.

Of course, there are several love puppies in the young-and-loaded set, but, as the reader will quickly discover, these desirous desirables are notoriously hard to get.

ALBERT VON THURN UND TAXIS
At $2.1 bil, his bankroll isn't very laaaaarge, but jet-set-born Albert, barely out of high school,

can bed any well-connected, kinked-out, couture-addicted, Brazilian-waxed aristocrat he might fancy.

GUY LALIBERTÉ

His $1.1 billion wad is even smaller than Albert's, but as cocreator and owner of Cirque du Soleil, he is most definitely billionairedom's hungriest party predator. If you want a bite of him, though, you'll find that your competition is a company of flamboyant and shapely acrobats. These ladies contort through the entire Kama Sutra before doing their squats. So brush up on your trampolining, hon.

ARNON MILCHAN

To seduce this 59-year-old fertilizer king/producer of *Pretty Woman*/Israeli arms dealer, you'd best, ho hum, be a leggy blonde no more than half his age, a requirement suggestively devoid of sexual imagination.

JEFFREY SKOLL

Easier for the average single person to bed: he's under 40 and lord of eBay. If you win your bid for him, you get to snuggle his Beanie Babies while screening the social-issue films he finances. With luck, he'll show you how he used to pump gas in Ontario, wink, wink.

RUPERT MURDOCH

Not all of the romantically active superrich are spring pheasants. In his early seventies, the tabloid chief recently managed to sire his sixth scion on his 36-year-old third wife. This studly feat makes Rupert's the most billionaireish sexuality of all, because, as any overlord can tell you, we top 1 percent were not put on earth to make love; we are here to make dynasties. — Maggie Cutler-Wages

Old-School Fun: Hunting Preserves

Just because it's farm-raised doesn't mean it's not wild

HEN YOU FEEL THE BLOOD lust rise, and even laying off an entire assembly line won't quench the urge, an African safari isn't your only release. The growing captive, or "canned," hunting industry was made to order for those of us born into the upper-crust hunting tradition.

Farm-raised game, unwanted zoo animals, even hand-raised endangered exotics are available at America's sports preserves for less than the price of an evening out in Monte.

There are more than 4,000 facilities across the US, the most popular of which are private, such as the Rolling Rock Club in Ligonier, Pennsylvania. Known to the masses primarily for golf, this 10,000-acre luxury club also has top-shelf fields and pens.

Since our pals at the Fish and Wildlife Service classify the killing of pen-raised animals on private lands as "harvesting," licenses, quantity limits, and seasonal restrictions are often not required or enforced. An aristocrat is limited only by trigger-finger cramps.

Lord of Your Domain

Colonel Kurtz Is Alive and Well

No billionaire would be content without a proper island vacation home. But why settle for just the house when you can buy the whole island, like Virgin founder Richard Branson, who counts a significant dot in the South Pacific among his precious commodities?

The analysis of island ownership must factor in the question of local political turmoil. But remember, what may be bribery in the American penal system is a mere gratuity (and a way of life) in the Third World. After all, what

continued

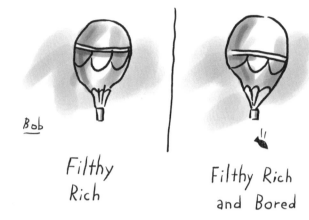

Bob

Filthy
Rich

Filthy Rich
and Bored

The trophy hunter can decorate the game room of a fourth or fifth home with the heads, pelts, or entire carcasses of exotics in a single afternoon—from the common lion cub, buffalo, kangaroo, ostrich, or zebra, to the soon-to-be-endangered Himalayan tahr, to unabashedly illegal endangered species.

One typically arrives by helicopter or limo in the appropriate camouflage (not that it matters, but costumes are so much fun). Depending on your hunting agenda, be it fowl or four-legged, some firearms may be too heavy for actually walking around, but a servant can hand you your piece when you find yourself face to face with your uncaged quarry.

Our hardworking VP, when not in an undisclosed location, has been known to jump into Air Force Two and fly out to pop a few hand-raised birds. Recently Mr. Cheney and nine associates slaughtered 417 out of 500 newly uncaged pheasants in one morning. (No word on how the other 83 escaped their death sentence; you can be sure it wasn't through a reprieve from the Supreme Court.) Dick plays as hard as he works: the morning's sport led to an afternoon of more shooting, this time in a duckly direction.

And just because we're shedding blood doesn't mean we can't spend some time furthering our plutocratic goals. Supreme Court Justice Antonin Scalia, though decidedly not a billionaire, enjoys similar perks, thanks to patrons and sometime litigants like Dick. These two hit it off when they did some male bonding and duck shooting in the swamps of Louisiana. (You can be sure His Honor got some thrills with our Dick close at hand, cruising on Air Force Two, trailed by yet another Air Force luxury jet.)

There are family-bonding opportunities, too. Young heirs and heiresses can build their own trophy collection as soon as they can pull a trigger. Imagine the envy of little Max or Maxine's playmates when they walk into your child's playroom and see the fresh, personally killed heads mounted on the wall. Kids will long honor and obey you for opportunities such as these.

The ultra-rich have enjoyed the comfort of gratuitous violence for millennia. In these fast-paced modern times, we mustn't lose sight of that. It doesn't require either marksmanship or a license, so go ahead—enjoy a day or even a ten-minute release (animals can be drugged into a docile stupor on request). You've earned it.

— Alan Greenspend / John McGarvey

is the likelihood that your high-priced white-collar criminal counsel can't beat an overreaching US Attorney coming after you for a violation of the Foreign Corrupt Practices Act?

Benefits abound for traveling and investing in Third World economies. Imagine—when you multiply your billion dollars by the ex-change rate in Bora Bora, you'll become an über-billionaire. Moreover, baksheesh in these economies is much more efficient than in the civilized world. When the price of an election is less than $8 million, the pur-chase of that zoning variance will sting only as much as your Christmas bonus to the club golf pro.

— Count de Monet / Wylie Stecklow

Planning the Billionoliday

Taking a break from the life of leisure

Have You Considered ... Easter Island?

Located approximately halfway between Ecuador and New Zealand and home to mysterious statuesque stone ruins, Easter Island has been drawing wealthy anthropologically bent travelers for decades. And since commercial air flights cost close to $1,000 minimum, it is a locale that only the wealthy can explore.

WHEN YOU LEAD A LIFE OF leisure, taking a vacation is no small feat. But sometimes one simply must get away from it all, regardless of how cushy "it all" is. One way to make the change of pace more evident is to declare a holiday, rather than a mere vacation. Or better yet, a Billionoliday!

SPECIAL BILLIONOLIDAY TRAVEL DESTINATIONS

Bhutan: Forget the conventional $30,000 trek up Mount Everest in neighboring Nepal. Shangri-La, commonly known as the Kingdom of Bhutan, has an unyielding policy of protecting its land from the tramplings of foreign visitors through the restrictive and extremely limited number of high-priced visas it issues each year.

Abu Dhabi: The King of Abu Dhabi has created a desert oasis through a concerted effort to invest hundreds of millions of dollars in unique architecturally designed hotels, five-star dining experiences, and world-renowned sporting events. All rooms have both CNN and Al-Jazeera on cable.

Peru: Machu Picchu has lured an international crowd of curious travelers since its rediscovery in 1911, but the recent find, just a few miles away, of another set of Inca ruins has created the opportunity for the über-wealthy to hire a crew of local Indians to carry you through overgrown forests to experience a unique adventure Billionoliday.

Cuba: Although the administration continues to support the wealthiest Cubans by restricting American travel to this island just a hop, skip, and jump from Florida, our pal Dubya has allowed a few exceptions to these travel limitations. The billionaire's Cuban visa is just a few well-placed dollars away. Live like the wealthy of the 1950s. Rent out the entire Hotel Nacional, and reinforce your view of the success of capitalism by taking a firsthand view of the failures of socialism.

Monte Carlo: Once regarded as the prerequisite destination for anybody who considers himself anybody of means, it's now hopelessly passé, but you might consider stopping by during the annual yacht show. It's an unparalleled opportunity to compare size.

Once you've chosen the destination, most of the rest will take care of itself (with a little help from your personal assistant). Yet the crucial choice will remain: wife or mistress? Husband or personal trainer? (Do us all, and the gossip mill, a favor. Choose both.)

— Count de Monet / Wylie Stecklow

❝❝ I know nothing about sex because I was always married. **❞❞**

— Zsa Zsa Gabor

Show Me the Money

Mating tips: don't settle for a millionaire

● **Don't limit yourself.**

It's just as easy to fall in love with a billionaire as a millionaire. Hey, why buy the horse when you can get the whole stable, and perhaps the OTB concession?

● **Don't be blinded by Cupid.**

Remember: love makes fools and paupers of us all. There will be plenty of time to date the bad boys and poets once you've got the big rock.

● **How handsome do you need?**

Think about it: you won't be seeing a lot of the man. If he's the kind of cash bull you're looking for, he'll be too busy making more money to hang around with you much.

● **Hot head = cold cash.**

A short-tempered CEO means a lot of smashed martini glasses, but you'll get plenty of make-up presents in return. The downside? This may involve dressing up as Alan Greenspan for make-up sex.

● **Follow the money.**

And watch where he spends it. If he squanders

it on golf courses rather than diamond mines, move on and hock that tiara on your way to the Bahamas. If not, tackle your prenup like a three-hour power brunch.

• Think geriatric.
Octogenarians will talk less, won't be able to remember your spending sprees, and often wind up taking the dirt nap before you can say "personal trainer." Plus, you can put them to bed at 8:00, go to the spa, and then paint the town green.

• Charity begins at home.
Learn to differentiate between self-hating billionaires who donate to lost causes like world peace and those who know how to capitalize on a savvy nonprofit charity. You've got a lifestyle to keep up.

• Verify.
You wouldn't buy a pure-bred Cavalier King Charles Spaniel without checking the pedigree, so don't head for the altar without making sure his papers are in order. Hire a good private eye; it's worth the investment.

• Just because he's rich doesn't mean he's not cheap.
Sure, you want him to use every tax loophole, but don't let him put you on a short leash—even if it is diamond-studded. Insist on your own unlimited credit lines.

• Finally: don't forget the escape valve.
Keep at least one penthouse in your name, and don't give him the address.

— Jill Weiner and Dara Colwell

Personal Assistant, Butler, or Servant?

The working poor in our estates

ORGIVE US FOR BEING ALARMIST, but for just a moment imagine a world where you don't wake to the sound of curtains being gently drawn and the appetizing aroma of rare wild salmon and strawberries on your breakfast tray. Instead, only the harsh buzzing from an "alarm clock," and no food except what may or may not be in the kitchen (somewhere downstairs).

This could happen if you were to lose control of your servants. Until indentured servitude returns fully to the USA and the EU, a billionaire needs to keep abreast of the economic realities of the working class living among us.

Domestics will remain one of the few groups yet to be outsourced, and not due merely to inconvenient etymology. But it's a different world altogether once you leave the States or the Continent. For your estates in Asia, child domestics are still quite popular, and legal in many countries. Children can be sold, borrowed, given, or bonded into domestic work. Keep your eye out for representatives of a group calling itself Anti-Slavery International. They are a bit of a nuisance, even for the less wealthy who enjoy this valuable child commodity. Remember, "many tiny hands make light work," and not just in sweatshops.

Some have suggested that automation will bring us robotic servants that will require no sleep, food, or messy emotions—the perfect slaves. But is it not their very emotions that hold our domestics so dear to us? Where is the pleasure in humiliating servants of steel? Where is the ego in this automated equation? The best practical use of such future steel-collar workers would be only as a threat to the help: "Don't make me automate your job."

— Alan Greenspend / John McGarvey

"Daddy, where do billionaires come from?"

Slumming It

Survival tips for adventures among the middle class

ES, IT'S POINTLESS BEING wealthy if we don't get to live in our own special world. But once in a while, perhaps even inadvertently, we find ourselves out with the middle classes, mixing and milling and fending for ourselves. Some consider it bracing and invigorating; to others, it's a nauseating and terrifying experience. For both types, we offer some tips on getting by when you're just another one of them.

Drinking beer from bottle: Purse lips, press bottle to them; gently allow liquid to flow into mouth. As bubbles may go up nose and cause choking, be sure to execute will in advance. Do not extend pinkie finger. Audible belching is encouraged.

Using microwave: Insert food item, enter cooking time (begin with 30-second increments), press "start." Do not use china with embedded gold or precious metals.

Ordering fast food: Keep it simple. Almost all outlets provide hamburger, french fries, and soda. There are no waiters. Stand at the counter near the center of the establishment and order from the cashier. Caveat: *do not eat.*

Opening milk carton: Follow arrows on top end of carton. If three attempts fail to yield the milk, consider another beverage—cognac perhaps.

Opening car door: Locate handle. Outside, often a silver or black bar; may require key. Inside, often above armrest; may be painted to match interior.

Changing flat tire: Let's not get carried away. Phone for replacement limo.

Using cash: Place goods on counter at register. After the total due has been announced, place bills on counter in front of clerk; larger denominations may cause ire and delays. Tipping is not required when paying at a cash register.

1. Locate desirable parking space.

2. Line up Hummer with spot.

3. Proceed into space.

ADVANCED—FOR INTREPID BILLIONAIRES ONLY!

Grocery shopping: Release single cart from row of shopping carts. Drive between aisles until desired goods pass nearby. (Do not attempt to search for specific items.) Look for items marked "ready to eat." Once items are selected, proceed to one of several checkout lines.

Public transportation

Subway: Each municipality has its own system, but usually there is a clerk sealed inside a plastic booth. Pay this clerk and ask for directions. Once on the platform, stand away from edge. Do not look at track bed or at fellow passengers.

Bus: You must pay upon entrance. Coins may be required. Each bus has its own fixed route. The driver will most likely not deviate from this route for less than several hundred dollars.

— Ike Horner de Marquette / Matthew Roth

"And one cooks with a hibachi? Umm.
The middle class tickles me so."

The Sleep of the Privileged

Upper-crusty nightmares

Being outrageously wealthy brings on ailments and burdens that the middle classes can't even dream of—and we're not just talking about gout. As you ascend the ranks of privilege, you'll notice your nightmares acquire a different cast. To help you feel more comfortable with the new dream world, here are a few examples of what to expect:

• Your trophy wife leaves you for the wife you left her for.

• You can't get the Hyundai off the bumper of your Hummer.

• You commission a renowned landscape architect to do a sculpture of your family, and he does your teenage daughters in cherry blossoms.

• The stockholders in your software company discover that business casual isn't just the way you dress on Friday but the way you do your job Monday to Thursday.

• The government brings back debtors' prisons and puts the executives who run credit-card companies in them.

- Your mansion is lifted up by a tornado and dropped downwind from your poultry-processing plant.

- You have had so much exercise and plastic surgery that you're made into an ice sculpture at Dennis Kozlowski's birthday bash.

- Robin Hood comes back from the dead to run the enforcement division at the Securities and Exchange Commission. And his office is within bow-and-arrow range of your executive washroom.

- You're a telecommunications magnate and you get trapped in the elevator with the cable guy.

- Your $3 million tax rebate wasn't deposited directly into your overseas account but came in the mail as Monopoly money.

- You go to sleep on your private jet and wake up on a commercial carrier. That's not all: you're in coach, and you're the only flight attendant.

- You go marlin fishing and wind up at the Red Lobster.

- One of your plastics factories poisons thousands of people, gives them cancer, causes birth defects, the usual. But it's in the US!

— Jill Weiner, Matt Reiss, and Jon Dellheim

Sort the Suitors

Telling the Gold Mines from the Gold Diggers

IS YOUR PROSPECTIVE SON- OR DAUGHTER-IN-law going to be an asset or a liability? Are they ready to be robber barons, or are they planning to rob you barren? Slip them this quiz over brunch at the club and find out!

1. So, when was your last trip to the Caymans?

a) I log on every morning to place my bets and chat with lonely men and women.
b) I go every year around April 14 and December 30.
c) Cayman Islands—where's that? (followed by a wink)
d) Dude! Spring break!

2. Complete this sentence: "Boarding schools are good places . . ."

a) For the parents and the children.
b) For the parents who hate children.
c) To meet other kids like us.
d) To sow wild oats.

3. What do you have to offer a potential employer?

a) Youth, beauty, and arrogance.

Maximizing Your Matrimonial Worth

Just because a diamond is forever doesn't mean the marriage has to be. We recommend a biannual assessment of the value of a matrimonial union vis-à-vis one's own potential on the open market. It can be a very savvy move to trade in short-term mating success for a long-term, bankable investment.

Timing is crucial. One wants to disengage and marry upward when one has the highest potential to snag the big prey. Fortunately, the rich are getting richer, which

continued

b) I am willing to fire my friends, and I know how to spot peculiarities in people's personnel records.

c) Contacts up the wazoo.

d) My fiancée.

4. What does NPR stand for?

a) National Pretentious Radio

b) National Pinko Radio

c) Not Popular Radio

d) National Police Radio

5. A few years after you marry, you notice your spouse has put on a few pounds. What do you do?

a) Pay someone to do her in.

b) Pay someone to do her.

c) Pay someone to do me.

d) Bite the bullet.

6. Which of the following does not belong in the group?

a) Pioneer

b) Frontiersman

c) Ranger

d) Maverick

7. Your fiancée has been offered a pre-IPO stake in one of the hottest new technology companies in the country. You do the due diligence for her and learn that its Eastern European factory employs four 1-year-old Romanian orphans continuously generating random patterns of movement copied into an operating code to protect it from outside encryption or manipulation. What do you do?

a) Say, "Where is my pen?"
b) Laugh heartlessly.
c) Suggest ways the company could find four more.
d) Move up the wedding date.

8. Would you consider appearing on a reality television show?

a) If it's called *Who Shot Donald Trump?*, I would.
b) If I could get new boobs, I would.
c) If I could own and produce it, I would.
d) If they'll put your son alone on a desert island, I would.

9. Complete this sentence: "I give to charities because . . ."

a) I get favorable tax deductions.
b) It makes me feel good.
c) President Bush told me to.
d) I love their balls.

10. Complete this sentence: "Prenuptial agreements are . . ."

a) We don't plan to get married—that's so bourgeois.
b) A sign that one of you has a lot more money than the other.
c) A sign of *respect*.
d) A sign you don't love me.

is superb news for Gold Diggers. Former seven-figure spouses are adding zeroes to their fortunes like never before. But keep in mind that this isn't teen romance. Upgrading spouses demands upper-bracket tactics.

Remember that capitalism is about turning luxuries into necessities. If you're wearing Vivier pumps and sleeping on Fretté linens, don't flash your Vogel thong to just any millionaire. Do the math before you switch meal tickets, or you may find yourself riding back from Dick and Dubya's next soirée on a commercial carrier!
— Dara Colwell

Remember: don't rely entirely on attire, diction, or the rumor mill to verify your child's potential mate. A good private investigator is a good private investment! Good luck and good will hunting!

ANSWERS

1. Gold Mine: D. A wise-guy answer like that is definitely a sign of a billionaire, or president of the United States, or, God willing, both. B shows initiative but not of the same magnitude. C, still not bad.

2. Gold Mine: Any answer, as long as it comes quickly. A hesitation indicates unfamiliarity with boarding-school philosophy.

3. Gold Mine: A, B, and C are the billionaire trifecta.

4. Gold Mine: B. That's the party line! Quaint use of archaic terminology shows pluck.

5. Gold Mine: D. Gold Digger: A, B, C, occasionally D.

6. Gold Mine: B. He or she knows that Rangers, Pioneers, and Mavericks are all categories of fundraisers collecting individual donations for the Bush campaign (Rangers, $200K; Pioneers, $100K; Mavericks, $50K). Clearly our kind of person. Gold Digger: A, C, or D. But since he or she doesn't even know the basics, probably not a very good Gold Digger.

7. Gold Mine: C. We have a winner!

8. Gold Mine: C. Thinks of all the angles. Gold Digger: B or D. Thinking of how much he or she can wrangle is admirable, but not this early in the game.

9. Editor's note: This question is included only to help disguise your intentions with this quiz. Of course it's not possible to distinguish between a Gold Mine or a Gold Digger with these answers. These are the reasons everybody gives to charities.

10. The best answer depends on the other answers. If your child's potential spouse is a Gold Mine, D is preferable. If he or she is a Gold Digger, A and C. For both Mines and Diggers, the wrong answer is B (this degree of honesty should raise a red flag). — **Hilary Hull and Jon Dellheim**

TGIF That HMO!

A glossary of middle-class terms

FINANCIAL TERMS

Pocket money: Funds remaining after rent, utilities, child care, insurance, taxes, etc., have been paid. Now largely replaced by revolving consumer debt.

Coupon: A scrap of paper offering a discount on the purchase of food or other item the consumer would not otherwise intend to purchase. Not to be confused with fixed-income assets, such as zero-coupon bonds.

HMO: Health-maintenance organization. A health-care delivery system that allows access to a restricted list of physicians who are willing to play by the rules. Individuals who can afford nothing better are encouraged not to get sick or have an accident outside the coverage network.

LABORERS' TERMS

Work clothes: Garments worn while working by employees who dress differently while not working.

Home-cooked meal: Food prepared in the residence by members of the family unit and consumed around a table or in front of a television. As no moneys are exchanged for services, not to be confused with victuals produced by live-in chef.

Car pool: A means of commuting between work and home in which workers take turns with the driving responsibilities. Much like having one's own driver, though less responsive to commands and more likely to stop for fast food or doughnuts.

Manual labor: Any work for hire not involving a computer or pen and paper.

Day care: Paid collective care of children while parents are working to pay the day-care bills. Not to be confused with a collective of children used in offshore manufacturing.

Maternity leave: The time off that a female worker is sometimes allowed to take for the process of giving birth to a child and recovering. In many places required by law.

Paycheck: Bimonthly credit doled out to employees to ensure purchasing power of consumer base. Traditionally issued on Fridays as boon to beverage industries.

TGIF: "Thank God It's Friday." An antiquated term, used when employees earned enough to work only 40 hours a week, often with only one member of the household providing income. In that era, Friday was traditionally the last day of the workweek.

MISCELLANEOUS TERMS

Studio apartment: A tiny, single-room, box-shaped worker (or artist) dwelling. Generally the next step up from an actual box on the street.

Answering machine: A device that receives incoming phone calls and records a message from the caller. Used in homes and offices without full-time staff and/or servants.

Gym membership: The fee for use of a worker collective of exercise devices, often used to relieve the stress acquired working for the upper classes.

Coach class: Formerly steerage. The area behind the curtains on a non-private plane. — Ike Horner de Marquette / Matthew Roth

Recommended Viewing

Movies we like (or don't)

BILLIONAIRE THUMBS UP

The Sting: Dress the part and people will give you money.

Pretty Woman: Finally, a positive spin on prostitution.

Breakfast at Tiffany's: We like anything at Tiffany's.

The Great Gatsby: Who cares if he dies? It's the lifestyle!

Indecent Proposal: Demi Moore for a million dollars? That's what we call good bang for the buck.

Oliver: This whole movie just plain makes sense.

Wall Street: Reveals too much, but we like the milieu.

Trading Places: Charming fantasy fun.

Melvin and Howard: A generous portrait of a generous man.

Arthur: He's a bit soft on the hired help, but he's one of us.

BILLIONAIRE THUMBS DOWN

Citizen Kane: Get over the sled—enjoy your money!

Scarface: A great business model gone horribly, horribly wrong.

Titanic: "My Fiancée Fell In With the Pool Boy."

Erin Brockovich: To be honest, we liked Julia Roberts better as a whore. **Gone With the Wind:** Why dwell on the downside of war? Frankly, my dear, we don't give a damn.

— Hilary Hull, Jill Weiner, and Jon Dellheim

The whole life of an American is passed
like a game of chance,
a revolutionary crisis, or a battle.

— ALEXIS DE TOCQUEVILLE

Chairman of the Board

The true story of Rich Uncle Pennybags (a.k.a. Mr. Monopoly)

FACTOID
Maximum number of US firms whose 2001 profit exceeded the combined profits of Native American casinos: 16.

FACTOID
Ratio of the combined annual revenue of Native American casinos to that of Las Vegas casinos: 5:3.

WHO WEARS A TOP HAT TO jail and collects $200 every time he passes Go? From his legendary hotel complexes on Boardwalk to countless bank errors in his favor, Rich Uncle Pennybags (a.k.a. Mr. Monopoly) hauls in an estimated four wheelbarrows of funny money every minute of every day in board games played around the world.

But few people living today know the shocking history behind the eleven-by-eleven-square world where he makes his billions.

The "official" story is as follows: Charles B. Darrow of Germantown, Pennsylvania, invented the game during the Great Depression. At the time, Darrow was an unemployed failure, having lost his sales job due to the stock-market crash of 1929.

It was a difficult time. Billionaires everywhere were forced to give up such necessities as third yachts and fourth country estates, while Darrow was a regular Horatio Alger who took "odd

jobs" to make "ends meet." Darrow also created puzzles and games, including Monopoly, which he drew on a kitchen tablecloth.

It all sounds so delightfully quaint and ruggedly entrepreneurial, but the truth is that our man Darrow did not invent Monopoly. No, thinking like a billionaire, the plucky little ducky appropriated the concept from a popular folk game and sold it as his own.

Apparently this isn't woolly-headed slander. An economics professor from California, Ralph Anspach, proved this charge against Darrow and Monopoly in a 1982 court decision that was later upheld by the Supreme Court of the United States.

The real history of Monopoly begins with a Quaker woman named Lizzie J. Magie, who in 1904 invented a Monopoly-like game that she patented as The Landlord's Game. Unlike Monopoly, this disturbing game mocked the accomplishments of billionaires with dismissive place names like Easy Street and Lord Blueblood's Estate.

The Landlord's Game also had an educational purpose—to teach players about the inequity of land monopolization that allows a few speculators to become superrich while others end up penniless. Sounds good to us, but one is suspicious of Magie's motives.

Magie based her game on the odious "single-tax movement," which advocated taxing land speculators to death. (Not to be confused with the fabulous "flat tax," which aims to give billionaires and clever monopolists a tax cut at the expense of the middle class.)

The single tax, which inspired Magie's game, was the brainchild of a rabble-rouser, Henry George, who bellyached about the monopolization of land resources. George's *Progress and Poverty* became one of the

Pennybags Saved

Over the years, Uncle Pennybags' name has changed, from "Rich Uncle" in the 1940s to "Mr. Monopoly."

Out of deep respect for the history of billionaires and our traditions, we continue to think of him as our own Rich Uncle Pennybags.

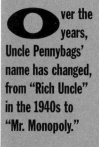

bestselling books of the nineteenth century, with its gripe that economic progress was benefiting too few and creating poverty and inequality for too many.

With this off-the-wall message behind it, The Landlord's Game survived into the 1930s. Players often modified it by creating new rules and hand-drawn game boards. Over the years it was sometimes renamed Auction Monopoly, or simply Monopoly.

A Pennsylvania hotel manager, Charles E. Todd, claimed he taught the folk monopoly game to Charles Darrow in the early 1930s. Fortunately for billionaires, Darrow took the game and made it his own, in one of the most delicious hostile takeovers in history.

Darrow sold Monopoly to Parker Brothers in 1935, and since then more than 200 million games have been sold, including over five billion tiny green houses. Darrow went on to become a semi-worthy millionaire in his own right, thanks to royalties. Since the 1930s approximately 500 million people worldwide have played Monopoly, unwittingly absorbing its pro-billionaire message.

That's right—like The Landlord's Game, Darrow's Monopoly is an educational tool. A testament to the timeless lesson that we in the ruling classes learn every day in the marketplace: getting rich at the expense of others is good, clean fun!　　　　　　　　— Drillmore Wells / David Hyde

EDITOR IN CHIEF
Kurt Opprecht

DEPUTY EDITOR
Matthew Reiss

CONTRIBUTING EDITORS
Jon Dellheim · Hilary Hull · Elissa Jiji
Kavita Kulkarni · D. M. Rider
Jeremy Varon

CONTRIBUTING WRITERS
Andrew Boyd · Abigail Caplovitz
Marco Ceglie · Dara Colwell
Maggie Cutler · Dave Daly
M. P. Dunleavey · Scott Faucheux
Jason Grote · David Hyde
Richard Lingeman · John McGarvey
Alice Meaker · Ken Mondschein
Patrick Nash · Miyong Noh
Victoria Olson · Adam Penenberg
Matthew Roth · Wylie Stecklow
Clifford Tasner · Jill Weiner

ART DIRECTOR
Bob Eckstein

DESIGN AND PRODUCTION
Christopher Lione

COPY CHIEF
David Olivenbaum

COPY EDITOR
Thomas Leonard

RESEARCHERS
Ben Maurer · Tanya Elder

CONTRIBUTING ARTISTS
John Kascht · Eric Palma · Mark Tuchman

Illustrations and icons by Bob Eckstein
unless otherwise noted

This book was produced by
Billionaires for Bush
Chief Executive Officer, Andrew Boyd

Thanks to John Oakes
of Thunder's Mouth Press

STANDARD OIL GOVERNING RULES
www.nationmaster.com/encyclopedia/Standard-Oil.
CHAPTER I
CONGRESS *Freshman class:* Associated Press, December 25, 2002; "Millionaires Populate U.S. Senate," CNN.com, June 13, 2003. *Top spenders won in 2000:* "Money Wins Big in 2000 Elections," Center for Responsive Politics, November 8, 2000. *Loving Those Lobbyists:* "Lobbyists Bankrolling Politics," Center for Public Integrity, May 18, 2004. *K Street Goes Elephant Alley:* Nicholas Confessore, "Welcome to the Machine: How the GOP Disciplined K Street and Made Bush Supreme," *Washington Monthly*, July/August 2003.
PAGE 21 *Federal lobbyists:* PoliticalMoneyLine (www.fecinfo .com). *Discretionary spending:* Congressional Budget Office.
FRACTIONAL OWNERSHIP OR PRIVATE JET?
NetJets: www.netjets.com.
PAGE 35 *Saudi ambassador:* George Bush Presidential Library and Museum. *Self-made:* Forbes magazine. *TV ad:* Advertising Age. *Debt for college tuition:* College Board.
HACKING AN ELECTION *Touch-screen machines:* Election Data Services, www.electiondataservices.com/home.htm. *Help America Vote Act:* Federal Election Commission, fecweb1.fec.gov/hava/hava.htm. *O'Dell:* Paul Krugman, "Hack the Vote," *New York Times*, December 2, 2003. *Easy to "hack":* "How E-Voting Threatens Democracy," Wired.com, March 29, 2004. *Hagel:* "Hagel's Ethics Filings Pose Disclosure Issue," *The Hill*, January 29, 2003. *Texas, Florida, Iowa:* "Can We Trust These Machines," Black Box Voting, black-boxvoting.org.
PAGE 37 *Vote producing no paper record:* Election Data Services.
PAGE 39 *Campaign contributions:* Center for Responsive Politics. *House and Senate incumbents:* Center for Responsive Politics. *2002 congressional race:* Center for Responsive Politics.
PAGE 44 *George W.'s tax cuts:* Citizens for Tax Justice (www.ctj.org).
BILLIONOCRACY *Bribes to Nigerian officials:* "Another Halliburton Probe," MSNBC.com, February 4, 2004.
THE WHITE HOUSE EFFECT Chuck Collins, Chris Hartman, Karen Kraut, and Gloribell Mota, *Shifty Tax Cuts: How They Move the Tax Burden Off the Rich and Onto Everyone Else* (United for a Fair Economy, 2004).
MAKING BILLIONS FROM YOUR GOVERNMENT POSITION *Rumsfeld study for Gingrich:* Rumsfeld Commission, "Report of the Commission to Assess the Ballistic Missile Threat to the United States," 1998 (www.fas.org/irp/threat). *Defense Policy Board:* Center for Public Integrity. *Feith and Zell:* Michelle Ciarrocca and William D. Hartung, *Axis of Influence: Behind the Bush Administration's Missile Defense Revival* (World Policy Institute, 2002).
JUDICIOUS INVESTING "The New Politics of Judicial Elections 2002," Justice at Stake Campaign (www.justiceatstake.org); PBS *Frontline* documentary, "Justice for Sale," 1999. *Is "buy" too crass:* "Trouble in Brooklyn Spurs Court Reforms," *New York Law Journal*, April 25, 2003. *Kennedy and Breyer:* "Is Justice Undermined by Campaign Contributions?," www.opensecrets.org. *Putting judges on retainer:* "Payola Justice: How Texas Supreme Court Justices Raise Money from Court Litigants," Texans for Public Justice, 1998 (www.tpj.org). *Texas judges think contributions affect outcomes:* "Justice Knows Fieger's Not the Problem," *Detroit Free Press*, September 22, 2003. *Reports suggest cash works:*

"Insurance Industry Contributed Heavily to New Justice's Campaign," *Akron Beacon Journal,* Novem-ber 11, 2003. *Broader empirical underpinnings:* "Pay to Play: How Big Money Buys Access to the Texas Supreme Court," Texans for Public Justice, 2001 (www.tpj.org). *North Carolina:* "High Court Defends New Judges' Code," *Raleigh News & Observer,* October 16, 2003.

PAGE 55 *Eight million workers lost overtime:* Economic Policy Institute.

HOW DO WE LOVE THEE, GEORGE? *Medicare profits:* Boston University School of Public Health, Health Reform Program (www.healthreformprogram.org). *Da juice:* Taxpayers for Common Sense (www.taxpayer.net). *Media consolidation:* www.fair.org/media-woes. *Five media companies:* Ben Bagdikian, *The New Media Monopoly* (Beacon Press, 2004). *Revenues of over $100 billion:* "The Big Ten," *The Nation* (www.thenation.com/special/bigten.html).

PAGE 57 *Lucrative (if useless) defense contracts:* "Bush's $396 Billion Military Budget: Leave No Defense Contractor Behind," Common Dreams (www.common-dreams.org). *Failed to pay $3 billion:* "27,000 Defense Contractors Owe Taxes, GAO Finds," *Washington Post,* February 12, 2004.

TAXING WORK, NOT WEALTH Chuck Collins, Chris Hartman, Karen Kraut, and Gloribell Mota, *Shifty Tax Cuts: How They Move the Tax Burden Off the Rich and Onto Everyone Else* (United for a Fair Economy, 2004).

CHAPTER II

LESS THAN ZERO "Study Finds Resurgence in Corpo-rate Tax Avoidance," Institute on Taxation and Economic Policy press release, October 19, 2000; "Tax Me If You Can," PBS *Frontline* documentary, February 2004; "Bush's Aggressive Accounting," Paul Krugman, *New York Times,* February 5, 2002; "The Decline of Corporate Income Tax Revenues," Center on Budget and Policy Priorities, rev. October 24, 2003.

BILLIONAIRES' CODE OF CONDUCT: INSIDER TRADING SEC safe harbor: www.law.uc.edu/ CCL/34ActRls/rule10b5-1.html.

REMEMBER YOUR NORVIR *NCDDG grant:* "Govern-ment Funding of Norvir/Ritonavir," essentialinventions.org. *Intellectual property:* "Abbott Defends AIDS Drug Price Rise to Panel," Reuters, May 25, 2004. *Raised price:* "Daily HIV/AIDS Report," Kaiser Family Foundation, April 27, 2004 (kaisernetwork.org).

A BILLIONAIRE'S GUIDE TO THE UNIVERSE Dan Briody, *The Iron Triangle: Inside the Secret World of the Carlyle Group* (John Wiley, 2003); Oliver Burkeman and Julian Borger, "The Ex-Presidents' Club," *Guardian,* October 31, 2001; Melanie Warner, "The Big Guys Work for the Carlyle Group. What Exactly Does It Do?" *Fortune,* March 18, 2002.

WHAT MONEY? David Cay Johnston, *Perfectly Legal: The Covert Campaign to Rig Our Tax System to Benefit the Super Rich—And Cheat Everybody Else* (Portfolio/Penguin, 2003). *Paul O'Neill:* "Bush, After Gaining Tax Cut, Now Takes Aim at Tax Code," *New York Times,* July 16, 2001. *Harken:* "Bush Co. Went Offshore," *New York Daily News,* July 31, 2002.

PAGE 87 *Richest 1 percent:* Citizens for Tax Justice (www.ctj.org).

PAGE 89 *62 environmental standards:* Robert F. Kennedy Jr., "Crimes Against Nature," Natural Resources Defense Council, November 21, 2003. *Officials resigned:* "Another EPA Official Resigns in Protest Over Bush Policies," Nat-ural Resources Defense Council, July 25, 2002.

PAGE 92 *EPA to NASA:* House Appropriations Com-mittee. *Oiled seabird:* Study by Brian E. Sharp, Ecological Perspectives. *Pollutants in blood and urine:* Environ-mental Working Group.

SCORCHED-EARTH RETAILING "Wal-Mart, a Nation Unto Itself," *New York Times,* April 17, 2004.

COVERING YOUR ASSETS *Gosman:* Congressional Record, www.senate.gov/~kohl/homestead.html. *Warner:* "Rich Debtors Finding Shelter Under a Populist Florida Law," *New York Times,* July 25, 1993. *Bilzerian:* "Owing $100-Million, Bilzerian Jailed Again," *St. Petersburg Times,* January 31, 2001. *Reynolds:* "Reynolds Gets Out From Under Bankruptcy," *Palm Beach Post,* October 8, 1998. *Texas:* "Bush Opposes Limiting Texas Bankruptcy Shelter," *Washington Post,* July 18, 1999.

PAGE 102 *Detroit and Saddam:* Office of the Mayor, Detroit. *CEO severance:* The Corporate Library, February 27, 2003.

THE ETHICIST *Harken:* Paul Krugman, "Succeeding in Business," *New York Times,* July 7, 2002. *433,333 shares:* "Cheney's Halliburton Ties Remain," CBSNews.com, September 26, 2003.

MAKING A LIVING MAKING A KILLING *Pyongyang:* Arms Control Association newsletter, June 2003.

CHAPTER III

BILLIONAIRES IN BED *Albert, Laliberté, Milchan, Skoll:* www.forbes.com/maserati/billionaires2004/cz_bill04_eli-gible slide.html. *Murdoch:* www.abc.net.au/am/s777043.htm.

OLD-SCHOOL FUN "Stacking the Hunt," *New York Times,* December 9, 2003; "Hunting Made Easy," *Time,* March 4, 2002. *Cheney and pheasants:* "Cheney in Region for a Day of Small-Game Hunting," *Pittsburgh Post-Gazette,* December 9, 2003. *Scalia:* "Scalia Was Cheney Hunt Trip Guest; Ethics Concern Grows," *Los Angeles Times,* February 5, 2004. *Young heirs:* www.suwanneeriverranch.com.

PAGE 120 *CEO to worker's salary:* www.ceogo.com. *CEO average salary: BusinessWeek,* February 9, 2004. *CEOs motivated: St. Louis Post-Dispatch,* March 26, 2004.

PAGE 122 *Fair Labor Standards Act:* U.S. Department of Labor, www.dol.gov/esa/whd/flsa.

PERSONAL ASSISTANT, BUTLER, OR SERVANT? Anti-Slavery International, www.antislavery.org; Child Workers in Asia, www.cwa.tnet.co.th.

PAGE 124 *Hummer:* White House, *Harper's* magazine. *Shoplifting:* University of Florida Security Research Pro-ject. *Lap dances:* Las Vegas Dancers Alliance.

SORT THE SUITORS *Rangers, Pioneers, Mavericks:* "President Bush's Run for the Money," editorial, *New York Times,* October 16, 2003.

CHAIRMAN OF THE BOARD *Official Monopoly history:* www.hasbro.com/monopoly, www.monopolycollector.com. *Folk monopoly history, Magie's story:* www.antimonopoly .com. *Pennybags:* www.boardgamegeek.com/game/3554, www.toonopedia.com/pennybag.htm.

PAGE 137 *US firms vs. casinos: Fortune* magazine, *Time* magazine. *Native American casinos vs. Las Vegas casinos:* National Indian Gaming Commission, Nevada Gaming Commission.

Seriously, though . . .

Are you a Billionaire for Bush? If not, you could be. Billionaires for Bush is a do-it-yourself street-theater and media campaign coming to a swing state, a city, a house, a you near you.

We use humor, savvy messaging, and cutting-edge internet organizing tools to flush out the truth about the Bush administration's disastrous economic policies and help turn the fat cats out of power in November and beyond.

As we go to press, there are 50 Billionaire chapters across the country. Check the Full Chapter List on our website, www.BillionairesForBush.com, for details. No chapter near you, you say? Consider starting your own!

Envious of our wealth and political muscle? You too can join the ranks of the filthy rich as we don our finery and take to the streets. Whether privatizing your local public library or taking part in an upcoming National Day of Action, you'll find all the materials you need in our Do It Yourself Kit. It's full of organizing tips, downloadable materials, songs, and more.

We need to take our nation back, and humor is one way to do it. It is a uniquely powerful weapon; help us wield it well.

Please join the campaign by lending your voice, your talent, your energy, your support. Thank you.

www.BillionairesForBush.com